How Can You
Defend
Those People?

Dedicated to the kids:

Jamie, Mark, Dani, Jacob, Josh, and Emily.

And to Ray Cushing, my mentor who taught me how to really listen to clients; my mom, Edith Sherman, who showed me that anything is possible if you believe in yourself; and *most of all* to Lis, who taught me, by example, and inspired me, with kindness and love, to be a better person.

{Contents}

Some names have been changed to protect the
innocent, the possibly innocent, the not-so-innocent,
**and to generally reduce the number of people
who may get pissed off at me.**

{Acknowledgments}

"Write a book? I can't even read a book." That was my standard response to any suggestion by a great many people over the years who suggested I write something. I finally took the shot, and with the continuous support and encouragement of my wife, Lis Wiehl, it became a reality.

I thank Carol Mann, my literary agent, for believing in me and introducing me to Gene Brissie of The Lyons Press who totally "got me" from day one. His encouragement, guidance, and support continues to be overwhelming and so appreciated. I thank Jenn Taber, editor extraordinaire at The Lyons Press for her patience in dealing with someone like me, who had no clue about this business.

I thank my lawyers and accountants for being there for me in so many ways: Willie Dow, Kathy Keneally, Allen Kosowsky and Neil Berkow.

I thank my agent/manager Lynda Bensky, who refused to believe that lawyers on TV could never get paid!

I thank my assistant, Luisa Carella, who can never do enough to try and make my job easier.

I thank Judy Jacobson, who believed in me a very long time ago and hung in there with me for most of a lifetime. Her support has always been very important.

I thank Roger Ligon for the privilege of being his lawyer.

Lastly, I thank *"those people"* who I have had the privilege to represent over the last 37 years. I hope this book demonstrates my appreciation to all of you who have placed your trust in me. I hope I will continue to be worthy of it.

{Introduction}

EVERY CRIMINAL DEFENSE ATTORNEY GETS IT. We walk into a cocktail party, bar mitzvah, PTA meeting, or the Motor Vehicle Department, and we're confronted by someone who comes up to us with the question: "Please don't take this the wrong way, but . . . how can you defend those people?" Before I can launch into our rehearsed speech, which talks about the Constitution, Clarence Darrow, and the Henry Fonda character in the movie *Twelve Angry Men*, they pull a Helen Thomas move and come right back with the obligatory follow-up: "I mean, how can you represent someone when you know that they're guilty?"

Generally, by this time, others have joined in on the conversation and are nodding excitedly, anticipating that we will either flip out like Sean Penn hitting the paparazzi or simply melt like the Wicked Witch of the West, having been doused with water. I take a deep breath and quickly glance at the crowd, sizing them up. Do they get the Barry Sheck Innocence Project speech? Maybe a rundown of Sacco & Vanzetti, the Scottsboro Boys, the Duke lacrosse fiasco, and some local case where some innocent guy got screwed? Then again, a simple "Up yours . . . Where's the bar?" might just be in order.

I am sick of apologizing for what my colleagues and I do. This book is *not* an apology in any way. Rather, it is an explanation and a response to all of those questions or complaints that we get every day. I am sure there are more questions out there, and this book may in fact encourage more whining, but I have to start somewhere.

{Chapter 1}

What! Me? Lawyer?

"You're a criminal defense lawyer? Wow! How can you do that work? I guess that is something you always wanted to be? You really deal with the filth of society!"

Everyone seems to have their own idea of how criminal defense lawyers are invented. Many of us were former prosecutors. Many of us (not me) have known all their lives they were destined for this mission. But what we all have in common is the red-and-white bull's-eye target on our backs. We are the Erich von Stroheims of the legal world—we are the lawyers you love to hate! . . . until you need us!

I rarely fight back when someone takes a shot at me for having chosen to be a criminal defense lawyer. Not long ago I was giving my standard "Confessions of a Criminal Lawyer" speech to a large group of retired men who were very sharp and asked me excellent questions. They all seemed to get it, and there was no hostile reaction to my explanation that I am in the business of sometimes allowing and assisting guilty people to go free. However, there was one guy in the front row who glared at me most of the time and obviously was not a fan. He didn't laugh at my jokes or appreciate my opening icebreaker: "Everyone, regardless of their race, religion, or ethnic origin, is entitled to be presumed innocent until proven broke!" How can you not laugh at that line? He didn't even smile.

When the question-and-answer period started, he was the first to raise his hand. "Mr. Sherman, you seem to be in the business of making these plea-bargain deals all the time in serious cases. If I raped somebody, what kind of deal would you make for me?" What the hell was he talking about? Where was he going with this? I fell back on what I know best and answered him without missing a beat. "I think I could get you a suspended sentence for assault with a dead weapon!" Big laughs—and he even liked it.

Over the years I have developed a pretty thick skin about other people's issues with my occupation. I would always write off their sneers as simply ignorance of the process. It really didn't affect me personally. I thought I was virtually un-insultable. But then along came a really angry lady named Kathy Stewart. I better back up a bit and give a very brief but accurate account of how my life's path led to where I am today, and how I encountered Kathy Stewart.

I was raised a poor Jewish child in the slums of Greenwich, Connecticut. Okay . . . there are no slums in Greenwich. So let's make that the middle-class section of Greenwich, Connecticut. A few years ago I used that "slums" line in a magazine piece about me; I am still writing letters of apology to everyone in the neighborhood. (Note to Mrs. Morretti, Joyce Vidra, and the rest of the Byram, Connecticut, population—I was kidding then . . . and now.) I just can't resist using the "slums of Greenwich" line. Apart from getting a guaranteed cheap laugh, I am trying to make the point that not everyone from this town is a snotty, filthy-rich kid with big-time trust funds who walks around like their excrement doesn't stink.

My family lived in a relatively small house next to a river. My father died when I was fifteen, and my mom worked several jobs to put my brother, sister, and me through college. One of my mother's jobs was pretty interesting. She was a personal assistant (before anyone ever heard of personal assistants) to famed opera and Broadway star Ezio Pinza. Pinza starred in the Broadway hit *South Pacific* and was a very nice man who was a larger-than-life character. Since I was on my own a lot, I kind of did my own thing. Actually, I performed a valuable service to the neighborhood. When the river/pond on our street would freeze over, my friends' parents would know that the ice was safe to skate on TWO WEEKS AFTER MICKEY SHERMAN WAS SKATING OUT THERE!

I grew up pretty much unsupervised, but managed to stay out of trouble, using my inappropriate but generally effective sense of humor to get me through any problems. My sixth-grade class picture essentially captures my youth, along with my philosophy of life: I am the very short kid with the red shirt sitting in the front, WITH MY BOOK CLEARLY UPSIDE DOWN! If you look closely enough, you can actually see the excitement in my soul, knowing that everyone would get a big laugh out of this when the pictures were distributed in a few weeks. Getting in trouble with the teacher and principal was easily an acceptable price to pay for this stroke of comedic genius.

My book continues to be upside down.

I was about three feet tall (or so it seemed), and my only real objective in life was to pass the height line at the roller-coaster ride at nearby Rye Playland Amusement Park. Growing up on the "mean streets of Greenwich," I was always the smallest kid in the class, and one of the very few Jews. I never got beat up or suffered from any anti-Semitism. I had the best time. Growing up as a "have not" in a very "have" community was fine with me. In Greenwich, the No Child Left Behind policy meant that everyone went to Nantucket during the summer and Vail during February vacation.

The town of Greenwich had great schools, parks, and beaches. The rich kids I knew had great houses, cars, and boats, and it never seemed to bother me much that they had a hell of a lot more than me. I hitchhiked to Tamarack Country Club every day during the summer to caddy. The bags weighed a thousand pounds and I hated being a galley slave, but the ten bucks was terrific! Besides learning to play golf on Mondays (caddy's day), I learned that it was infinitely better to be a *member* of a country club than to carry other members' crap around. The bottom line is that I was neither bitter nor jealous of the rich kids—just hopeful and somewhat determined to be one of them someday.

I spent four terrific years at Greenwich High School, where my biggest disappointment, upon graduation, was being barely edged out for "Class Clown." I did win "Most School Spirited," which is nice . . . but not as nice (to me) as Class Clown. My strong "C" average somehow got me into the University of Connecticut, where I continued my academic mediocrity, majoring in *Having a Real Good Time*. I did okay on the law boards and somehow got into the University of Connecticut Law School. This was 1968, and the draft board seemed to have other plans for me.

Although I had gone to college during the height of the Vietnam War and the drug revolution, both were of little interest to me. I tried marijuana twice and hated it because you had to share the soggy wet thing with other people. And as far as the Vietnam War was concerned, I seemed to be far more concerned about whether our fraternity's ice sculpture was being properly built by the pledges, not unlike a scene from *Animal House*. (I was in the "Omegas"—the guys with the blue blazers, led by Greg Marmalard in the movie.)

I took the army physical and, incredibly, got rejected at the last station when some doctor poked my stomach and told me I had an enlarged spleen from having had mononucleosis. So—off to law school. Why law school? Why not? I really wish I had this great story to tell about why I chose to go into law—that I saw some injustice and pledged my life to do good. Didn't happen. All my friends were going to law school, and it just seemed like a good idea at the time—even though I never really fit in there. As in the sixth grade, I basically hid under the desk, hoping not to get called on. After the first year I worked full-time as a substitute civics teacher at a nearby school and managed to pass by doing fairly well on the exams.

My third year of law school did have an impact on me. I left substitute teaching to work as a clerk in the Superior Court in New Haven, Connecticut. The city of New Haven was filled with police officers and federal agents, and the stores were boarded up with plywood. At that time, one of the notorious Black Panthers, Bobby Seale, was on trial for murder. I essentially went AWOL from my job at the courthouse and spent every moment I could watching that trial. Both sides were incredible; I was really impressed. The state's attorney for New Haven County, Arnold Markle, was as professional and polished as one could imagine. Seale was defended by Charles Garry of San Francisco. Garry was methodical and infinitely clever. What impressed me the most about him was his ability to speak brilliantly yet never sound like a lawyer. The case ended with a mistrial after the jury hung. The judge, showing incredible courage and chutzpah, dismissed the case, not allowing the State to take another crack at convicting Seale. He essentially said that the State took their best shot and this community had to move on. Watching Garry, I really did kind of get religion. I wanted to be a criminal defense lawyer and do what he did.

When I graduated from the University of Connecticut Law School, my signature "C" average did not prompt dozens of law firms to romance me. I got a job clerking at the local Superior Court, where I spent four months sufficiently kissing up to the judges to be appointed a full-time public defender when that job opened up. Generally speaking, being a public defender sucks. Don't get me wrong: Public defenders don't suck—quite the contrary. These lawyers are the unsung heroes of the criminal justice world, who get paid very little to work tirelessly to help clients who do not trust them enough to tell them the truth. Their resources are generally very limited and are often dwarfed by the vast powers of the prosecution, who can pick up a phone and have an agent, cop, or detective do this or that.

The caseload of the public defender is often scary as well. When Mark Geragos was the lawyer for both Scott Peterson and Michael

Jackson, scores of people expressed shock that a lawyer could handle two such big cases at the same time. In the world of the public defender, this is the norm. In fact, most public defenders have several "big cases" going on at the same time, together with umpteen "not-so-big cases." The measure of a good defense lawyer, public or private, is to effectively let your client know that you understand his not-so-big case is just as important as the one that makes front-page news.

The PD suffers from the most difficult public relations problems imaginable. First, most people believe you get nothing for nothing. If their lawyer is not charging them any money, how good can their services really be? If they were really good lawyers, they would be "real" lawyers, out there making some decent money. This last complaint always gets to me. In point of fact, most public defenders could *absolutely* make a damn good living out in the real world. They wouldn't have to put up with the crappy work conditions, and they could buy nicer cars and wear better suits! So why don't they do that? Because they generally *care* about doing "God's work" in this system, and they want to make a difference in the lives of the poor souls who can't get up the five thousand bucks to hire Joe Blow . . . or Mickey Sherman. You cannot put a value on their personal level of commitment to their profession and to their clients.

So, why don't the public defenders' clients trust them? Consider the traditional scenario: You get arrested by the police, who work for the *State*. They bring you to the *state* courthouse where the *state* prosecutor puts you in front of the *state* judge, where you are informed of the fact that you are charged with various violations of *state* law. But, not to worry—they give you a lawyer! Who comes out? Some guy who works for the *STATE!* The clients are entitled to be paranoid!

Finally, it is a fact of life that the public often identifies the lawyer with his client. My boss and mentor during my stint as a public defender was an incredibly decent man named Ray Cushing. Ray often said that we public defenders, "on the social scale of life, were only one notch above our clients who cannot make bond!" Sadly, the clients and the public are not the only people who sell the public defenders short. To make matters worse, there are some *judges* who refuse to accord them the respect and civility they deserve. They view the legal efforts of the public defender as some type of collaboration with the enemy, the defendants.

The best example of this unfair and perverted attitude occurred in 2007 in the municipal court of Portage County, Ohio. A judge threw a public defender in jail for contempt of court after the attorney said he was unprepared for a trial. Did he delay the trial for years in some slick weasel move? Not exactly. The public defender had been appointed to represent the man for assault charges THE DAY BEFORE! The judge demanded that the public defender conduct this man's trial after having had the case for less than twenty-four hours. When the public defender, Brian Jones, rightfully refused to sell his client so short by trying a case with *no* preparation, the judge ordered him taken into custody in front of his client, the spectators, and courthouse personnel.

Sometimes judges do stupid things, and later, upon reflection, back off and try to make things right. Not Portage County's judge, John Plough (that's right—I am using his real name, and hoping that I don't get caught speeding on his turf in Ohio)! After this incident received a great deal of national media attention, Judge Plough responded with: "The public defender's office is not going to impede justice in Portage County." Yikes! Somebody call the nearest village and find out if they're missing an idiot! Of course, the hero of this story is Brian Jones, who, in the tradition of the much-maligned public defenders, chose to go to jail rather than participate in a perversion of the criminal justice process.

We criminal defense lawyers watch out for each other. We belong to the National Association of Criminal Defense Lawyers (NACDL). When we meet at various hotels around the country, I often get a kick out of the people who come out of the wedding in the Wisteria Room and glance at the hotel events board, which announces that we are there. They move away faster than the jailers in *Ben-Hur* did when they discovered that Charlton Heston's mother and sister had leprosy. When Mr. Jones was locked up, Carmen Hernandez, president of NACDL, issued a press release condemning the trial judge's actions for violating the right to effective assistance of counsel. Her words are very much worth reproducing here.

> For the jury or judge to find the truth at trial, the defense must understand the case and be prepared. Defense lawyers must have investigated, talked to the witnesses, researched the law, and, frequently, consulted experts. Indeed, defense attorneys are required to do these things by a long line of U.S. Supreme Court precedent and the ethical rules that govern lawyers in every state in the Union.
>
> Asking a lawyer to go to trial without preparation is like asking a doctor to perform surgery before diagnosing the patient. Harm is inevitable; the facts will be unclear and evidence will be missed. Worst of all, the wrong people may go to jail while real criminals remain at large. We ought not to forget so quickly the lessons that the Duke lacrosse players who were falsely accused of crimes taught us.
>
> For the scales of justice to be balanced, both the prosecution and the defense must be prepared. Without this balance, mistakes happen. We deserve and are entitled to better than an unreliable criminal justice system. Public defenders must be given the time and resources to do their jobs.

Her lecture here seems to be very much suited for a speech to someone who came here from Borat's Kazakhstan, or maybe another planet. It is incredibly scary and sad that she had to explain these principles to Judge Plough.

I spent a year as a public defender and learned a great deal. I learned a little about the law, but mostly about dealing with people in crisis. Ray Cushing had an uncanny ability to listen to people nobody else seemed to give a damn about. These people had serious personal problems and were charged with committing the vilest acts, for which they were usually totally guilty! Not only had they been arrested before, but they were also the children and grandchildren of Ray's clients.

Ray rarely opened a law book and didn't try a lot of cases. What he did do, and do better than anyone I have ever encountered in "the system," is *care*. Clients would tell him the most bizarre stories or offer up the most absurd explanations for their conduct, which would embarrass Baron Munchausen. They would appear in the lockup on Monday morning after Ray had gotten them out of jail on Friday, having committed another stupid act against Ray's advice and in spite of his efforts. Ray would gently smile and ask them to explain what happened, offering his reassurance that he understood why they had hit their husband over the head with a frying pan. He was an island of comfort and confidence in a world that often seems to be designed to dehumanize and put down the very people who find themselves being pushed through this sausage factory. I vividly remember Ray explaining to another public defender that we may be the only people in our clients' lives who take the time to listen to what they have to say, and to accord them a measure of dignity and respect. It was and still is an invaluable credo.

A great lawyer is someone who can at least *appear* to give a damn. Ray not only gave that appearance; he truly did care. He also had an uncanny skill for finding *something* good or positive about any given client, and even more important, he was always able to articulate this in court. As a judge once said to me, Ray "could make chicken soup out of chicken feathers." There was another judge, Sarsfield Ford, who loved to terrorize Ray day after day in the courtroom. When Ray would put forth his sanitized version of his client's absurd bullshit story, this judge would lay into Ray as if Ray himself had committed the crime. Ray would always hold his ground, but it was like watching a baby seal being clubbed to death on the Discovery Channel.

Judge Ford called me when he found out I was organizing Ray's retirement party years ago. He not only wanted to attend—he wanted to speak. Many thought he was going to crap on Ray, but I knew better. Judge Ford was extraordinarily tough but also very fair, and, unbeknownst to most people, he had a terrific sense of humor. (He is a die-hard Notre Dame alumnus and fan, and knowing this, I once borrowed someone's Notre Dame letter jacket and had my client wear it during his sentencing. The client was a crack dealer who clearly knew nothing about Notre Dame. The judge smiled ever so slightly but went on to do his thing.)

On another occasion, I was representing someone for something that Judge Ford would have been very tough on if my client were to plead guilty before him. He asked if I was ready to proceed in the case. I told him, in open court, that I needed a few weeks to research a particular issue. "What issue is that, Mr. Sherman?" asked Judge Ford.

"Your vacation schedule, Your Honor." (This brought gasps from most everyone in the courtroom.)

"I can understand that. Granted . . . you have three weeks."

Sometimes it just pays to hold the book upside down! He thought it was genuinely funny, and honest, and rewarded me by allowing me to duck him.

When Judge Ford got up to speak at Ray Cushing's retirement dinner, there were still some people who thought he would be less than kind. What followed was easily the most touching and insightful speech about Ray's career. He told us that Ray Cushing was everything we could ever ask for in an attorney. Patient, kind, and knowledgeable, he inspired confidence and warmth in every client. He didn't care about making a splash; he cared about making people's lives better. No matter what happened to Ray's clients, they left the courthouse, manacled or not, knowing that their lawyer had done everything he could to help them—the best testament any lawyer could hear.

•••

After a year as a public defender, I heard there was an opening in the prosecutor's office. I had sufficiently sucked up to the judges during the past year, and they gave me the position. On Friday I was a lowly public defender who appeared to conspire with the dregs of society to make every citizen's life a bit of a nightmare by scamming the system and putting all the crooks back on the street. (Even my mother rarely took my calls.) By Monday morning, I had a much better parking space at the courthouse, and everyone greeted me like I had just emerged from the Publishers Clearing House van with Ed McMahon and a big check. At the hot dog truck, I was given VIP treatment. I was now one of the good guys . . . a prosecutor. In restaurants, everyone wanted to buy me a drink. It was as if I was Dorothy, and Toto and I had just woken up in Munchkinland. Everything was now in color, and I was no longer a scumbag.

Totally aware that this statement will piss off a lot of my friends, I can honestly say that being a prosecutor was the easiest job in the world. You wake up every morning and play God for eight hours. You have the power to make people's lives very miserable, or to grant them your mercy and take enormous burdens off their backs. What I learned early on about being a prosecutor is that I was a representative of the State, and that carried a fair amount of responsibility. The prosecutor has the unique power and responsibility to do the right thing. Sometimes that means prosecuting the hell out of a case. Quite often, however, it means righting the wrongs that may have been committed by the police.

In 1947, the great director Elia Kazan (*On the Waterfront*, *A Streetcar Named Desire*, *Gentlemen's Agreement*) filmed a movie called

Boomerang! in Stamford, Connecticut, based on the true story of a man who was accused of murdering a local priest. The real events actually occurred twenty minutes up the road in Bridgeport, yet the film people liked Stamford locations better. Dana Andrews played a character based on real-life local district attorney, Homer Cummings, a political rising star in the state who was a sure thing for governor. The story depicts the town being up in arms, demanding vigorous prosecution of the man charged with the crime. The problem is that Cummings's political aspirations were inferior to his innate sense of fairness. The night before the preliminary hearing, we see Cummings in his study, reading a law book. The camera closes in on a very tight shot of one line: *It is the duty of the public prosecutor not to convict, but to see that justice is done.*

The next morning, Cummings shows up in court, and in a terrific dramatic scene, proves that the defendant is innocent and that he will *not* prosecute the man. The movie's epilogue tells us that even though Cummings was not nominated for governor, he did become attorney general of the United States under FDR. The first-class law firm of Cummings & Lockwood still carries his name in Connecticut. (My daughter-in-law, Rachel Sherman, is a trusts and estates attorney there.)

Most prosecutors do their best to live by that credo, but sometimes they forget it and feel that everyone arrested *must* be guilty and therefore, should be prosecuted. The measure of a good prosecutor is often not how many of their cases result in guilty verdicts or pleas, but rather, how wisely they use their immense power of prosecutorial discretion. Occasionally, political and personal ambitions or insecurities cloud their judgment. No case better illustrates that than the Duke University lacrosse team disaster where three young men were hung out to dry for over a year because the prosecutor had obviously never seen the movie *Boomerang!* By not using his discretion when the facts clearly cried out for it, he made the worst of a bad situation. He has paid dearly for it by being disbarred, disgraced, and even briefly JAILED! The three young men and their families suffered through endless months of humiliation, public condemnation, and enormous expense. Yet, they were ultimately proclaimed innocent by the North Carolina attorney general, who had the good sense to do the right thing.

The real losers in the Duke lacrosse mess are the many actual rape victims whose testimony—as valid, justified, and truthful as it may be—will be disbelieved or discounted by juries who will be wondering if this is another "Duke situation." Like the Kobe Bryant case, the legacy of the Duke scandal is the dark shadow that will be cast over legitimate rape prosecutions across the country. This is a bigger problem than people seem to appreciate. What makes the North Carolina case so frustrating is how preventable it was: All that Mike Nifong had to do in the Duke lacrosse case was simply play by the rules—not such a tall order. Davy Crockett said (well, at least the Disney people *said* that he said): "Just be sure you're right—and then go ahead." It really is as simple as that.

With the exception of major felony cases, you really can't screw up too much as a prosecutor. Most defense lawyers like to say that trying a case as a prosecutor essentially consists of putting on a lot of cops and a victim and just saying, "What happened next?" I am not one of those backbiting, bitter defense lawyers. I believe prosecutors work exceptionally hard to achieve justice—especially all of those prosecutors who work at the Stamford, Connecticut, Superior Court. They are surely the best in the business, and deserve big-time raises and . . . all right—I have kissed their asses enough here. Maybe, just maybe, I won't get treated like crap the next time I walk into the courthouse. (Clearly, I have no shame or limits when it comes to brownnosing.)

But there is no denying that there is a very limited amount of pressure on the prosecutor. If you go to trial and lose, nobody really gets hurt too much. When the defense lawyer loses, our clients go to jail or get records, become forever branded as sex offenders or otherwise have their lives and those of their families screwed up. It might not be our fault, but we were the lawyers sitting next to them when the jury said, "Guilty." Very few of us can get used to that or accept it. When the prosecutor loses, nobody is pissed off at him. Assuming he did a credible job, even the victims will be okay with him. And it doesn't really matter that much, because he will get another shot when the guy gets arrested again, which is usually the case.

I was a prosecutor for four years. I spent most of that time trying various jury cases, which is really where the fun is. At Greenwich High School, I was the emcee and cowriter of the annual Senior Show, now called the SRO (Standing Room Only). Working as a prosecutor was essentially the same shtick. I got up in front of a bunch of people every day and entertained them. I tried to pick and choose the cases that I would take to trial. I was generally a pushover for a decent sob story, and I consistently threw a lot of the crap cases out. When it appeared that someone was going to be represented by a really good defense lawyer, I was inclined *not* to toss the case because I wanted to go to trial with the big gun and learn something. I often got my butt kicked in those situations, but the education I received during the ordeal was more than worth it. On reflection, I guess I was not the most diligent of prosecutors if you consider that someone's fate depended on whether or not he had the bucks to hire a lawyer whom I wanted to spar with.

I sometimes did have the opportunity to really help people who needed a break. At times I became an apologist for the police. Ray Cushing came running up to me in the hall one Monday morning, saying, "You'll never believe who's in the lockup!" I didn't have a chance to answer before he excitedly followed up with, "Claude Brown!"

I am not a big reader (I suffer from attention deficit disorder), but I knew who Claude Brown was. "You mean Claude Brown, as in *Manchild in the Promised Land* Claude Brown?" Ray grinned and held up his copy of Brown's prize-winning autobiography. Brown had grown up on the not-so-easy streets of Harlem, and told his story in this great

1965 book, which is still required reading for anyone who really wants to learn about urban issues and the real African American experience. Ray had gone home to get his copy for Brown to sign. The "overnighters" were not going to be presented before the judge until about noon. On any given Monday, there would be a dozen or so prisoners who were arrested over the weekend and were being presented for arraignment on Monday. Every criminal court around the country basically has the same routine: A human bracelet of men is marched in before the judge. They are often cuffed together, sometimes wearing leg manacles as well. They may have been arrested for anything from larceny to assault to rape.

The judge reviews police reports or affidavits and makes a finding of probable cause if he believes there is enough evidence to hold them. The issue of bond is then addressed. Unless we are dealing with a murder, the judge will set a bond that may be posted with cash or a professional bondsman. Some jurisdictions permit other forms of security, such as real estate or a 10 percent cash payment. The amount of bail is supposed to be a monetary amount that is sufficient to ensure that the person will come back to court. Many factors are taken into consideration, such as the track record of the accused in appearing in court for other cases; the seriousness of the offense; the safety of the public; and the accused's ties to the community. Generally, the seriousness of the offense and the length and nature of the prior record seem to be the prevailing issues.

Often, the bail is set by the police immediately after an arrest, and that bail is then reviewed (and often changed) in court by the judge. The good part of this situation is that the arrested person does not have to spend the night in jail because he can bond out within hours of the actual arrest. The bad part, however, is the tendency for the police to use the amount of bond as a carrot to convince people to confess to crimes, or more often, to "rat" other people out for various crimes. Clearly, the propensity of the accused to be an informant is not supposed to be a factor, or *the* factor, in determining how much money someone must cough up before they can get out of jail. Yet, in the real world, the police play this card very effectively. They also snooker people into giving up someone else by promising to keep the arrest out of the newspaper.

Should the defendant not make bond at the police department, he will find himself in court the next morning at his arraignment, where bond is then reviewed and set by the judge. There is a brief argument by the prosecutor, defense counsel (often a public defender), and perhaps another court officer, whose job it is to interview the prisoner and recommend to the judge an appropriate bail. The judge comes up with a number, and then the prisoner is ushered out, glancing over his shoulder to see if his "people" are in court, and whether they brought bail money or have made a deal with a bail bondsman to get him out.

When the prisoner does that slight pivot to check the gallery, that is the moment my tried-and-true theory kicks in. Over these many years I have observed this moment in court, and I've made the following observation, which I've dubbed *Sherman's Court Corollary*:

There is a directly inverse relationship between the disgustingness of the overnight prisoner and the hotness of the girl waiting for him in the gallery with money to bail him out.

I am very proud of this breakthrough revelation, even though I have not been asked to speak about it at any American Psychiatric Association conference or such. I have managed to mention it on several TV shows, much to the horror of the host. It never fails to spark interest—and several angry e-mails. Yet, ask anyone who finds themselves in any arraignment courtroom: When the guy with a four-page rap sheet, incredibly greasy hair, and sixty-five facial piercings comes out to be arraigned for having sex with a kitten, the hottest woman in the building sobs uncontrollably.

Okay—I know you are wondering what in hell this has to do with any serious criminal justice issue. Nothing really; if you feel guilty about reading so much about a silly issue, spend another twenty-five bucks and buy Barry Sheck's latest book on his Innocence Project! That should even things out.

One last story about an arraignment before finishing the Claude Brown story.

Many years ago when I was a prosecutor, I walked into the courtroom with the "overnight" files. There was only one: some guy who had molested a young girl somewhere. It was a very ugly case, and I was a bit concerned because there was a fifth-grade class taking up the first three rows of the gallery on a school trip to the courthouse. I had just finished my speech to the class. I always started with the same lines:

"So, what grade are you guys in?"

"Fifth grade!" one or two would shout back.

"Wow . . . fifth grade! That was the best two years of my life!"

Long, uncomfortable pause as the teachers snicker. Invariably I milk the joke in a bad Johnny Carson imitation. "Ya get it? Best TWO years . . . TWO years . . ."

Generally, I get big laughs from the teachers and parents who have brought the kids there, and that is enough reward for me. Then I answer their questions.

Q: *How do you get to be a court bailiff?*

A: You have to be able to sleep standing up with your eyes open, and make sure you are never around when the judge needs something.

Q: *What kinds of crimes are prosecuted here?*

A: Most people are here because they took those labels off mattresses and chairs that say, "Do not remove under penalty of law."

Q: *How do you get to be a lawyer?*
A: You have to be not smart enough to be a doctor.

Q: *Why does the judge wear that robe thing?*
A: Actually, it's a raincoat—the roof leaks over his bench.

I wish I could say that I am kidding about these questions and my answers, but I am not. I have taken great pride over the years in shocking the teachers and parents with my shtick. After both acknowledging the appreciation of the adults who laughed at my jokes and at the same time avoiding eye contact with those who were appalled at my irreverence and inappropriate sense of humor, the sheriff brought out the lone prisoner. I announced to the judge that the accused was charged with sexually assaulting a young girl. The prisoner looked like crap. He was cuffed behind the back, and the leg chains made him stoop over and walk very awkwardly. The kids in the gallery could not see his face, which seemed kind of appropriate to me. The judge began advising him of his rights. "Sir, are you John Smith and do you understand—"

"That's my daddy!"

One of the fifth-grade students was standing up and pointing at this poor soul. Tears were streaming down her cheeks as she kept hollering out, "Daddy . . . Daddy!" Soon, the prisoner was crying. Soon, I was crying; we were all crying. It was easily one of the worst moments I have ever experienced. The young girl was rushed out of the courtroom by her teacher and some parents. I ran through the arraignment process quickly and got the man out of there as soon as possible. I have long since forgotten what happened to him, but I will never forget that awful moment.

So the next morning Ray Cushing was standing in the courthouse hallway, waiting for the overnight prisoners, starring Claude Brown, to be brought up. I ran into my office and tried to find out what he had been charged with. Apparently he was on his way to the movies with a lady friend. A police officer stopped him "for a routine questioning," whatever that means. Brown was asked to show his license and registration. Brown asked why he was being stopped. The officer could not give any real answer other than some "routine *blah blah blah*." It was clear to Claude Brown (and to me) that he was being stopped for DWB—Driving While Black. He was a black man with a white woman in a late-model Cadillac. Some officer took offense at this and pulled him over to check him out. I had not seen this type of prejudice before in the local police department, and honestly, have not seen it too much since. Clearly this was an aberration, but that was of little consolation the next morning to Claude Brown. Why was he in jail? He was so outraged by the officer's conduct that, when told that there was no particular reason he was being pulled over, he refused to cooperate in any way. He would not hand over his license or registration. Accordingly, he was charged with these minor offenses and taken into custody, where he refused to post bond.

As I walked out of my office, I could hear the cacophony of handcuffs and leg irons coming down the hall. There were about ten prisoners, in a line of two abreast, handcuffed to each other. At the front of the pack was Claude Brown, who was handcuffed to Henry Jordan, the town drunk of forty years. Henry was the incarnation of Otis Campbell from *The Andy Griffith Show*, who used to get drunk and walk into the Mayberry lockup, open the cell door, lie down on a bunk, and go to sleep every weekend. Henry was a tall black man who was every bit as amiable as Otis, and just as well liked in the community. When sober, he would stop by the courthouse to bring candy and flowers to the ladies in the clerk's office. He was a nice man, sober or drunk.

The police once tried to scare him out of his drinking habit, using a somewhat unconventional and quite politically incorrect method. After booking Henry one evening, the officers discussed, *in his presence*, the fact that he had so many arrests that the chief had ordered them to form a firing squad and shoot him. They brought him outside the headquarters building and had him stand against a brick wall. At that point several officers lined up with their pistols pointed at him and counted down from ten to one, waiting for Henry to scream out and promise never to drink again. They had the wrong guy. Henry had apparently accepted the fact that he was about to be executed and calmly waited to meet his maker. Crestfallen, the officers told him his execution had been called off, and they put him back in the cell to sleep it off before his arraignment the following morning. As I said above, this was not a terribly orthodox method of dealing with Henry's drinking issue. Were it to happen today, and the press found out about it, Al Sharpton would be in front of the courthouse before you could say "photo op."

Marching behind Claude Brown and Henry Jordan were a group of eight men charged with a gaggle of misdemeanors and felonies. I approached Brown and introduced myself as the prosecutor. I reached out to shake his hand. He slowly raised his hand and shook mine. Of course, I was also shaking Henry Jordan's hand at the same time, since they were cuffed together. This might have been one of Henry's finer moments. He was not used to receiving such a welcome from the prosecutor! I had the bailiffs release Brown and I took him into my office. I did not ask him for his side of the story. I told him I had read the police report and it was obvious that the police had acted inappropriately. I explained that this was the exception and not the rule in this city, but I understood that this explanation did little to heal the very real injury to his dignity as a human being.

He told me that he was going to be writing the cover story for next week's *New York Times Magazine*. This incident might be a great basis for the story. *Uggghhh*. I told him that he did not need to go into the courtroom and that I would dismiss the charges in his absence. He wasn't smiling when he left the building, but neither was he taking names. As he left, he did manage to sign Ray Cushing's copy of *Manchild in the Promised Land*. As I said, being a prosecutor means you want to do the right thing. It is nice to have that power . . . as long as you use it well.

• • •

After four years of prosecuting, I had a problem. I was living in a condominium the size of a refrigerator box with my wife and two young children. The only way I was going to be able to buy a house in the area was to go out into the real world and practice law—or win a boatload of money on a TV game show. Naturally, I elected to go the game-show route. I appeared on two in New York and one in L.A. I learned that you can get on the shows if you can pass a trivia test and act like a genuine moron during the interviews and mock games. I have always been good with trivia, and acting like an extroverted moron, for better or worse, seemed to come naturally to me. When I filled out the applications, I always put down that I had incredibly interesting hobbies, like researching the Dead Sea Scrolls or ice climbing. The contest coordinators love to write this kind of crap on cards and provide them to the host, so they can make light banter during the introductions, or between games when they make believe as if they really give a crap about your personal life.

I made a few dollars on *Jackpot*, hosted by Geoff Edwards, a genial man who probably owns more plaid leisure suits than anyone else on the planet. I screwed up when I couldn't answer *What card game is found in a fireplace?* (poker). I was then the champion for three and a half days on *The $20,000 Pyramid*. I won several thousand dollars but got screwed when my celebrity partner disqualified us with one clue left to go in the "winner's circle." She was trying to get me to say, "Thing found in the sea." Her final clue (for me to win 20K) was . . . "Seaweed" (buzzer)! Dick Clark politely told her that the judges had disqualified the clue, and instead of the big money, I won the home game of *Pyramid* and some crappy dishes. (Thank you, Vicki Lawrence!)

A consolation "prize" from that show was getting a real big laugh. One of the games required my celebrity to get me to say, "Things you face." His clue: "You pray there." I quickly shot back, "The Wailing Wall." We won that game, and Dick Clark asked nobody in particular,

"Where is the Wailing Wall?" I responded, "Miami Beach!" Big laugh from Clark and lots of guffaws from the audience.

As a result of the game-show scandals of the 1950s, the FCC had ruled that each contestant could only appear on a total of three game shows in their lifetime. I had one left. The big money at that time was on *Jeopardy!* I know a lot of obscure facts, and I can think fast on my feet, but my grades throughout grammar school, high school, college, and law school reflected that a better match might be a show where knowledge might be *secondary* to the luck of spinning a wheel or something. Years later I learned that I was not the only TV lawyer to go the game-show route. Jack Ford, second to none in legal punditry, put himself through Fordham Law School on his *Jeopardy!* winnings. Before that, he went to Yale on a football scholarship. He is a *Jeopardy!*-qualified kind of guy!

After weighing my game-show options, I decided *The Joker's Wild* was perfect for me. Jack Barry, having risen like the phoenix from the game-show scandals, hosted a show where extroverted morons pulled a big slot-machine lever and then answered questions, competing with other extroverted morons for some decent cash and prizes. The show was in Hollywood, and I got on easily after having proved myself on the first two shows.

By this time I was a seasoned veteran of the game-show circuit. I had learned that the games really started in the green rooms and the practice sessions. Most of the contestants were new to public speaking, much less to being on television. I learned to prey on this weakness with offstage banter, such as: "The week that I was on *Jeopardy!*, the food wasn't as good as this!" or "Wasn't that nice of Mr. Barry to take some of us out to dinner last night?" The best psych-out line would come about forty seconds before we went on air. "Boy, there's about three hundred people in that audience out there, but I can't believe MILLIONS will be watching us on TV!"

I did well on *The Joker's Wild*. I was the champion for a couple of days, and I won a two-week trip to Hawaii. (*Who was the wife of Ulysses?*)

I won a hot tub! (*Largest desert in Mongolia?*) I won about $17,000, and all kinds of crap like cleaning fluid, a camera, and a typewriter.

• • •

You can't buy a house in Fairfield County, Connecticut, for $17,000 and a lot of crap, so I had to leave the prosecutor's office and try being a real lawyer. I hung out a shingle and have been a criminal defense lawyer ever since. I left the prosecutor's office on a Friday and was in court with clients on the following Monday. Many local lawyers referred clients to me because they appreciated that I hadn't been a schmuck when I was a prosecutor. They believed that I would serve their clients well, which is all that counts. I tried a lot of cases and did pretty well with murders and rapes before juries. The success of a criminal lawyer's practice is based upon results; it's as simple as that. Advertising, brochures, Internet stuff—that might bring people in to the office . . . once. But you are only going to be successful when the community believes, with good reason, that you have the ability and track record to get the job done.

In 1989, I tried one of the first cases on Court TV. Having been the subject of a lot of media coverage, I soon became a regular on all the legal shows, which has become my "night job" over the years. The net effect of this media exposure and good fortune in my practice has been to make me a very visible character in the community. The good news is that I have done fairly well representing people accused of bad acts. The bad news is that some folks seem to have a problem with that.

Okay, here is where this Kathy Stewart comes in. Around the middle of April 2005, I received a call at my office from a nice lady who informed me that she was the director of student activities at my beloved alma mater, Greenwich High School. Would I like to be this year's graduation speaker? Of course I would, I said; but I suggested she wait a week to officially invite me, and in the meantime, that she make sure everyone at the school was on board with this idea. I told her that some people might not like the idea of a criminal defense lawyer sending their kids off into the real world. She assured me that this would not be the case, but still agreed to my "gestation" period before making it official.

A week later I got another call from her, confirming the school's desire to have me speak at graduation. This was followed by an e-mail that afternoon:

Mr. Sherman,
It was a pleasure speaking with you this morning, and I am so delighted that you are going to speak at graduation. I informed a few students, and their whoops of joy should demonstrate the tenor around GHS—we are all looking forward to seeing you, and we anticipate a wonderful graduation day.

The e-mail went on to tell me the schedule for the ceremony, a dinner I was invited to attend with the school mucky-mucks, and that I could bring guests. This was pretty cool. I am on TV several times a week and get to go to very nice events because I am a C-list celebrity—but this was very special. I would go back to my high school as the commencement speaker. I was very psyched.

I left the next day for Kansas where I had been handling a cold-case murder dating back twenty-three years. I was still in Kansas a week later when I got a call on my cell phone from the student activities director who had invited me and sent me the nice e-mail. "I'm really sorry about this," she began sheepishly, "but there is a problem with your DWIs."

My DWIs? Did she have some information that I had been charged with drunk driving? I asked her what she was talking about. She asked me if it was true that I had represented students from the high school for drunk driving. "Well, yeah . . . that is what I do. In fact, I have represented teachers and administrators from the high school for the same thing—and considerably worse. So what is the problem?" I said. I still didn't get it. She explained that some parents had complained to the administration and the newspaper that my speaking would send a bad message to the students.

"Maybe we can do it next year!" she said reassuringly.

"Sure!" I cheerfully responded. "Don't worry about it."

I hung up and went back to my Kansas trial. What I wanted to ask her is whether or not the powers-that-be had considered what kind of publicity or public reaction this might generate. Surely it was an embarrassment to me, but I really thought it might give the school a bigger black eye. The local newspaper had called me a couple of days earlier to confirm that I had been selected as the commencement speaker. I confirmed it, and gave them one of my clever and self-deprecating "upside-down book" quotes, which they didn't run. The story of my being selected never ran; it just wasn't that newsworthy. But a story about me getting fired and humiliated like an *Apprentice* contestant would be terrific news! I knew it, but I didn't think the Greenwich High folks did.

The next morning in Kansas, I got a call from my son, and law associate, Mark. "Congratulations, Dad! You made the front-page, above-the-fold headline!"

The headline read: GHS RESCINDS PLAN TO HAVE SHERMAN SPEAK TO GRADUATES, and the article went on to quote a woman by the name of Kathy Stewart, a mother of a GHS senior. In a letter of protest to the *Greenwich Time*, Stewart had written: "Unfortunately, regardless of what Mr. Sherman chooses as his theme on the occasion, his life's advocacy represents the quest for personal celebrity and the complete disregard for the importance of taking responsibility for the choices in one's life." This one woman had single-handedly gotten me fired from speaking at the graduation ceremony! But, to make matters worse, the article included quotes from GHS headmaster Alan Capasso (who stated that my invitation to speak was premature), and ended with my wise-ass comment that would have been really funny . . . if I hadn't been dumped!

"I'm honored to be asked," said Sherman, who grew up in Byram. "I was shocked. It is a victory for mediocre students everywhere."

"Okay," I assured my son. "It's bad, but at least it's a *one-day story.*" (After all, I consider myself a media expert . . .) Meanwhile, Mark told me that he thought he knew who this Kathy Stewart was; he had done some tutoring for the SATs in Greenwich, and thought that he had taught her son for a considerable period of time. It turns out he did. How big a scumbag could I be if she allowed her son to be tutored by my son! Should I give this to the newspaper to take a shot at her? Naaahhh . . . I will keep to the high road (at least until I write a book . . .).

As we say in showbiz, cut to the next morning, where I am answering my cell phone in the Kansas courthouse lobby again:

"Dad, I voted for you—twice!"

"What the hell are you talking about?"

"Check out today's paper online."

The local newspapers, *Greenwich Time* and Stamford's *The Advocate*, were running a daily Internet poll in the community, asking people to vote on whether or not I should be the graduation speaker. The poll (complete with a picture of me sneering) appeared on the front pages of both papers for three days, as well as on their websites. So much for my "one-day story" theory. I was asked again to respond to this Internet voting story. I stuck to my game plan and answered with, "Hey—if I get over 80 percent of the vote, maybe I can speak at Brunswick!" (an elegant private school in Greenwich). I sensed that my wisecrack public responses were not making the high school people very happy. Obviously, their happiness was not high on my priority list at that point.

I assured Mark that this latest Internet thing was fine. It was still a local story that would die fairly quickly. Again, cut to the next morning, with me looking at my cell phone with a pained look on my face as I see my son's number once again.

"Okay . . . what do we have today?"

Mark had just two words to tell me. "Page Six!"

The lead story on the gossip-laden Page Six of the *New York Post*! I had beat out Paris Hilton!

Three days later, *The New York Times* picked up the story, and GHS headmaster Alan Capasso took another shot at me. "Many felt that due to Mr. Sherman's controversial clients, having him speak would create controversy . . ."

But now things started to change. The local papers were being literally flooded with letters from people in the community, as well as GHS grads from around the country who follow the local news online. Everybody was really pissed off. One letter was better than the next. How could the school system cave in to one parent, who obviously had no grasp or understanding of the criminal justice system? One of my favorite letters to the editor was from a former police officer:

To the editor:

I was distressed to read about the controversy regarding Mickey Sherman speaking at the Greenwich High School graduation. I served as a police officer in Greenwich for many years, and suffice to say, policemen and lawyers often mix like oil and water. Mickey Sherman is the consummate professional. I have worked on cases with Attorney Sherman, and I have also come up against him in trial.

Yes, he might attempt to show that my investigation could have been more thorough, or that something that made his client look guilty could be taken another way. This is our system, and Mickey Sherman, more than any other attorney I ever observed, would do his job and do it well. He made you feel that you had done your job as a policeman, and he was doing

his as a defense attorney. I think all of us would want that in a lawyer,
should we ever find ourselves in a situation where we needed one.

I got supportive calls, e-mails, and letters from everywhere. Even
the newspaper weighed in, in a big way. They really understood me,
calling me "an unlikely martyr" who "seems attracted to the show-
business spotlight. Humility is rarely in evidence." Can't argue with
that too much. The editorial then went on to totally support me in
every possible way. I'm not used to being praised in the local papers,
but this was getting good. Thank you, Kathy Stewart! Finally I'm the
good guy! The letters continued, although I never heard from the
headmaster, Mr. Capasso. I don't know him, but I thought it was odd
that he never called to at least offer some form of apology or explanation or something. Instead, I awoke one morning to another call from
Mark. I didn't want to hear it.

"Don't tell me—lemme just look at the paper."

I had been replaced as speaker by Connecticut's attorney general,
Richard Blumenthal. A very close friend for about twenty-five years,
Dick Blumenthal needs three Sherpa bearers to carry his résumé.
Harvard undergrad, Yale Law, Supreme Court Clerk, United States
Attorney, *Washington Post* reporter, U.S. Marine, perennial favorite for
Connecticut governor if he wanted it—and worse, a really decent guy.
Why couldn't they have found some schmuck!

The next night Dick and I found ourselves on the same dais at a
roast for the first selectman of Greenwich. I find myself to be the butt
of most everyone's speeches. Dan Malloy, the mayor of Stamford, Connecticut, got big laughs (mine included) when he explained to the crowd
that, "When I read about Mickey Sherman in the Greenwich paper, I
just assumed he lost another big case!" My speech had nothing to do
with the first selectman. I thanked the school system for making me a
martyr, and then let everyone know that they only asked me to speak
because both Menendez brothers were unavailable. I then congratulated

our attorney general and very sincerely proclaimed that he was a "terrific second choice."

The next morning, the front page of the local papers featured a new Internet poll. Prominently displayed in a box on the front page were pictures of myself and Attorney General Blumenthal. Readers were directed to a Web site to vote for who was "The Better Choice" to be the commencement speaker. Remember, I am barely qualified to be Blumenthal's driver! Naturally, I am calling all my friends (an endangered species after all this crap) and telling them to vote, and vote often! After a couple of days the poll results come out. Where? Page Six of course! I win by half a percentage point! Victory is mine.

Dick ended up giving a terrific speech at the graduation and used my jab as his theme. He spoke about being a second choice and how the graduates will likewise deal with such choices in the future. It is not by accident that he has that forty-page résumé.

But in the end, Kathy Stewart won. Instead of calling me and asking me, "How can you defend those people?" she raised hell with the school and convinced them that *nobody* should defend those people, and if someone does, they are our dirty little secret who ought to be shunned and certainly not honored in any way. What was, and is, so comforting has been the reaction and total support of the community—not so much for me, but for the very basic principle that everyone deserves a defense. Yet somehow, the town, *my* town, just let it happen. That still stings. As much levity as I have tried to attach to the "Mickey Sherman Fiasco," it still bothers me, personally and professionally. Adlai Stevenson said it best when he lost to Eisenhower the second time: "I am too old to cry, but it hurts too much to laugh."

• • •

Recently, I was invited back to Greenwich High to join two police officers and my new best friend, the headmaster, Mr. Capasso. I was asked to talk to the parents and students about the legal consequences of drinking and driving. When the PTA president approached me to speak, she asked if I would agree not to mention the previous graduation speaker mess. I told her that I could never pass up the chance to make a joke. When I rose to speak to the assembly that night I thanked the group for inviting me and told them that I was a bit nervous when I took my seat up on the stage and saw the two uniformed police officers. "I thought they were here to throw me out!" Everybody laughed. Even Mr. Capasso kind of smiled. Kind of.

{Chapter 2}

How Can You Represent Someone When You Know That They're Guilty?

WE DEFENSE LAWYERS might as well be wearing "kick me" signs on our backs. People cannot wait to ask us this question. I sometimes think they expect us to respond with a tearful, "You're right . . . What the hell was I thinking?" What is always amazing to me is the transformation that people can undergo, suddenly changing from outraged or offended by what we do for a living, to supportive and understanding. This metamorphosis generally occurs precisely ten minutes after their son or daughter gets arrested. Then, they call to tell us of the gross injustice that has been perpetrated by some idiot cop who refused to believe that "some black guy" threw a bag of marijuana in their son's BMW after he took a wrong turn and was cruising near a housing project . . . But in any event, the question deserves to be answered.

Here's the first problem. How do I *know*? Okay, sometimes the client does come in and say, "I did it! I did exactly what they say I did, and I have no real defense!" This is rare, but it does happen. I will deal with that later in this chapter. Let's call those people the *Really Guilty Clients*. I have had clients who have been charged with crimes ranging from murder, rape, and robbery to stealing toothpaste from the A&P. Many of them have admitted to having committed the very offense for which they have been charged. They have told me that the police, eyewitness, or victim's account of their conduct is precisely correct. This is not the most common situation, but it does happen quite often. The knowledge that my client is 100 percent guilty neither offends nor shocks me. That is just the nature of this business. People do stupid or bad things. People like me are there to clean up the mess, or at least, to do our best to minimize how their conduct will impact the rest of their life.

This doesn't mean we will set out to commit some great fraud against the court, or encourage our client or his friends to lie about what may have happened. My absolute knowledge of the client's guilt merely limits our options. We cannot put the client on the witness stand and allow him or anyone else to lie about the situation. Aside from that, we can do everything possible to either win an acquittal by reason of the State's failure to prove their case, or work out some other plea bargain, which might prove to be a far better result for the client than he would have faced should he have gone to trial and lost.

The tough part is getting the client to actually open up and tell me the real story as soon as possible. Sometimes I have to act a bit like a poor man's version of Kojak to get the real story. Lying is sometimes useful. "Look, Frank, the prosecutor told me he has a video of you leaving the apartment house at three A.M. How do we explain that?" And bingo—out comes the real story. Later, I can tell him how the prosecutor was bullshitting me about the video. No good could really come out of my letting him know it was really *my* bullshit story to get him to tell me the real deal.

Oddly enough, the more educated, sophisticated, and affluent a client is, the *less likely* he is to tell me the real story. Go figure. Over the years I have found that the most effective way to find out what really happened with the client is not to ask him, "What happened?" but rather, to ask him, "What do *they* (those imbeciles who arrested him) say happened?" As often as not, when I ask the client why he has been arrested, he will basically tell me that the police must have picked his name out of the phone book because they were having a slow day! Well, not in those exact words, but the responses are often as ridiculous. When I phrase the question in terms of not *what he did*, but rather *what those idiots* say *he did* or *what his wife/girlfriend/miscellaneous victim says he did*, the real story generally comes out.

Sometimes the "real story" comes out in a different way. A friend of mine was once hired to represent a young man charged with drunk driving. The case was problematic in that the young man had made an official complaint of police brutality against the arresting officer. The boy claimed that the officer had punched him in the face several times during the booking process. The father of the accused was irate. His son had called him from the booking room when the officer was retrieving some paperwork. His son was very upset and angry that the officer was brutalizing him, and pleaded with his father to come down there immediately and save him from this thug in a uniform. When the father got to the police headquarters, his son had a swollen black eye and obvious swelling about his face. The father was very pissed off.

Weeks later, my friend was in court with his client. There was a question as to whether or not the young man had actually refused or consented to a breath test. In order to learn exactly what had occurred, the police had sent a videotape over to the prosecutor's office. Many police stations are equipped with video cameras to record the testing process of a suspected drunk driver, as well as to memorialize the defendant's precise response to the officer's request for a blood, breath, or urine test. In this case, for some reason, nobody had looked at the tape until the refusal of the test became an issue, at which time the tape was sent over to the courthouse. The prosecutor put it on as the young man, his lawyer, and his father watched.

The officer is seen and heard acting in an incredibly patient manner, doing his best to let the young man know his rights and trying to fill out his forms and finish the process. The young man, on the other hand, is nasty, disrespectful, uncooperative, and behaving like a total schmuck. At one point the officer leaves the room while the young man is sitting in a chair, not handcuffed or restrained. He obviously has no idea there is a video camera pointed at him. He calmly looks around and all of a sudden, punches himself in the eye with so much force that he falls over backward in the chair! He then gets back up and does it again. This time he grinds his fist into his face and eye.

The officer comes back in with some additional paperwork. Having no clue as to what has just happened, he asks the young man if he wants to submit to a breath test. The request is met with more obnoxious conduct by the young man, who now demands to speak to his father. The officer directs him to the phone and leaves the room again to give the prisoner privacy for his phone call. The young man continues to grind his fist into his face, which is now obviously swollen and red. When his father answers, we hear the boy telling him how he has been falsely arrested, and that the cop has been beating him up. The audio is perfect. The officer comes back into the room as the boy is finishing the call. The boy tells the officer that everybody's going to get sued here because of the officer's brutality. The cop basically smiles and chalks it up to classic bad behavior on the part of a classic drunk driver. He is used to this.

As the tape is removed from the VCR, the young man has nothing to say. The father looks at his son, but likewise can't bring himself to say anything. My friend, their lawyer, just shakes his head, trying very hard not to laugh. But the best part was yet to come: The prosecutor (or the police department) sent the tape to a TV tabloid show, which in turn ran the video a thousand times, nationally.

● ● ●

Most prospective clients know that whatever they tell us is privileged information and cannot be used against them. However, there is very often a slight pause as they look at me to see if I really *will* keep their story a secret. I can understand this. They don't know me. Why should they trust a stranger? Occasionally I have to remind them that it is unethical for me to "tell on them" to the authorities, and that I will take their confession with me to the grave. Every criminal lawyer knows that this is what we have signed up for, but sometimes it's not so black and white. More than once I've had to push the envelope with this issue.

I once represented a man for fighting with the police. The case was resolved, with the client getting probation and counseling but no jail time. The police reports reflected that he had been especially angry and disturbed when the confrontation occurred. It was a few notches above someone having too many cocktails and mouthing off. He clearly seemed dangerous, but thankfully, nobody really got hurt. I knew he often battled with his wife and they were in the process of, at the risk of sounding redundant, a classic ugly divorce. One morning he called me at the office.

"Mickey, this is Fred Miller; are you going to be in the office all day?"

A bit confused, I said, "Uh . . . yeah; do you need to see me for something?"

"No—I'm going to kill Betty this afternoon, and I know I will need you after I do it!"

Yikes! What do I do? Ignore it? Could he be serious? In his case, I knew his history, and I totally believed he was capable of doing something horrible here. He was a nice guy, but obviously had some serious demons working against him. He was *my* client. He had confided in me. Could I violate his confidence?

This was a very difficult situation, but it was a no-brainer as far as I was concerned. Lawyers are supposed to do whatever is necessary to *prevent* clients from committing crimes. Once they have done the deed, we are obligated to not rat them out! But if they let us know they are *going to* break the law, we may have an obligation to take measures to keep that from happening. To be honest, I was happy that I believed the law was on my side, but I think I would have done the same thing even if it had been less clear. I called the wife and her lawyer. I told them exactly what had transpired, and said that if they wanted to call the police, I would cooperate. My client ended up being committed to a mental institution for several months. When he got out, he called me to thank me for doing what I did.

My second story is not so neatly wrapped up in terms of what the rules may or may not dictate. I was called one night by the parents of a young man who was in police custody for allegedly committing a house burglary. He was in jail, and the parents asked me to go down there to take care of whatever needed to be taken care of. Generally, I just refer people to a bail bondsman at this point, and meet with them at the office sometime after they get out of jail. But in this case, the young man insisted that I come down there immediately. So be it.

When I do run down to the police station in these situations, I follow the same protocol: First, I let the officer on duty at the booking desk know that I am there, noting the time in their records. I then say that I want to see my client right away, and that if any questioning is under way, it should stop immediately. (This is important, as the police may be getting my client to confess while I am sitting on my butt in the waiting room.) After putting the brakes on any interrogation, my next step is not to talk to the client, but to the cops instead. More often than not, they will tell me what they think happened, and why my client is sitting back there in handcuffs. This information is crucial to any conversation I will then have with the client. He may be totally innocent, but it is imperative that I know *what* he is accused of having done. At that point, I ask to speak to the client. The police in my burglary situation told me that they had caught my client in someone's home after an alarm went off. They also said they believed he had committed other burglaries in the area.

No big deal. I went into a small cell and met with my client. He had a drug problem, which is why he had burglarized the home. He had no prior record, and his situation seemed somewhat routine. Drug treatment (some kind of rehab program), a suspended jail sentence with probation, and I'm outta here.

Not yet. He had something else to tell me. After looking all around to make sure there was nobody listening, he told me that he'd had a gun when he burglarized the house.

"Well, they didn't charge you with a weapon. I wonder why?" I said.

I was not ready for his answer. He told me that he'd had the gun on him when the police grabbed him, but somehow they hadn't found it when they patted him down. Even though he was handcuffed, he was somehow able to remove the gun from his pants and shove it between the seats *in the back of the police car!* Things went downhill from there.

"Was it loaded?" I asked.

"Yes—full clip."

Wrong answer.

"Where did the gun come from?"

"I robbed a house down the street from that one last week and got it there."

The Latin term for this legal dilemma is *Holy shit!*

I am now aware of a loaded gun that is sitting in the back of a police car, which is about to be used by some officer, whose job it is to put criminals in the back of the car when they do bad things. What are the odds that some really bad guy will soon be sitting there, find the gun, and shoot the cop?

What happens if I tell the police? First, I am exposing my client to a more serious charge in that the burglary has now been committed with a firearm. *And* I am totally screwing him because now he will be charged with another burglary, which the police have no clue he has committed—at least until I tell them about the gun, whose registration number will lead them to that home. This will all expose my client to a possible additional ten-year sentence.

Damn. Why did I ever leave the prosecutor's office?

I then asked my client what he wanted to do about this problem. He didn't know of any problem. They didn't find a gun on him and that was that. I don't blame him for taking that position. Why should he fall on any swords? I then asked him directly about his concern for the safety of the cops because of that gun being available to the next guy who got arrested. He was sympathetic but still very adamant that he did not want to be charged with more crimes here. I told him I understood, and then hollered to the officers to let me out of the cell.

I called his parents and told them the whole deal. Understandably, they took the same position. So now what do I do? I went home and started calling my criminal lawyer friends. They all repeated my "Holy shit" line. They also told me what I didn't want to hear: You cannot inform on your client! Determined to find a way where I could protect the police, my client, and my own ass, I went back to the police station. I asked to see the chief of detectives. A very no-nonsense guy, this officer had always impressed me with his common sense and total candor. I told him I had a problem that involved the safety of his men but required some real balls to deal with it—on both our sides.

I told him that I knew where a gun was that might very well pose a real threat to the safety of his men. The price for my revealing that location would be his promise not to charge my client with possession of that gun, or any other offense that might stem from the gun's discovery. The chief took about a minute to think about my proposal and then said we had a deal. I then told him where the gun was and how it got there. He thanked me and I went back home, wondering what it was going to be like applying for a job in advertising after my disbarment.

A few days later I appeared in court with my client. I read all the police reports that the prosecutor had been furnished with, and there was no mention of a gun or any other burglary. There was never a mention of the gun, ever. The chief of detectives kept his promise, and I was off the hook. The client received drug treatment and probation. He also straightened out after the court hearing and never got into any further problems with the law. My client was lucky. The cops were lucky. I was lucky. Clearly, I had violated the trust of the client and a number of ethical rules. I knew that, but I still took the shot. Sometimes things are not as black and white as we all would like them to be. Thus, while actual knowledge of my client's guilt is certainly helpful in figuring out how to best handle the case, it sometimes comes with some baggage that can be extraordinarily difficult to deal with.

• • •

How do clients find their way to my office? In the beginning, I found myself representing a great many of the people that I had prosecuted. This is not unusual. I was never mean-spirited or vindictive, and I always did my best to treat all defendants with respect. When I hung out my shingle, they came to me. I also found myself getting many clients through referrals from law firms that didn't want to dirty their hands with criminal cases. Soon, clients came to me because I had established a pretty good track record at the courthouse. They either heard or read about cases of mine that had worked out very well. I earned a good reputation, but also learned that it was not always so deserved. The public has a very interesting outlook on some lawyers. They love to love us and they love to hate us. How often have we heard someone literally brag about what a nasty son of a bitch his or her divorce lawyer was! That's right—bragging about the insensitivity or meanness of their divorce lawyer. Go figure.

In the criminal law business, the clients want to confirm the wisdom of their decision to hire us, so they frequently attribute great deeds to us that are often quite exaggerated, if not completely fabricated. I've had clients tell me they know of a case where I got a jury to find a guy not guilty after his seventh DWI arrest. I've had clients tell me they hired me because they heard about the rape case that I got dismissed because I tore the victim apart on the witness stand and had her arrested for perjury! Both never happened. When I tell the prospective client that I am not that good, and that the story they are relating to me, about me, is really bullshit, they just assume I am being modest. Whatever—when they write the check, it becomes a nonissue.

Interviewing clients often involves skills that one is not taught in law school. You have to learn a different language and a different way of interpreting what people say. Take, for instance, the common question: "Do you have a criminal record?" This seems like a fairly simple question, which shouldn't need much amplification. But when the client says, "No," you must follow it up with, "Have you ever been arrested?" The frequent response is, "Yes—but I never served time . . ." In other words, many people believe that even though they have been arrested and convicted of a crime, it doesn't really count as a "criminal record" since they didn't go to jail.

Similarly, the simple question "Did you give a statement to the police?" is often answered in the negative. When I see the police reports, I find out that the client clearly told the officers or detectives that he *had* committed the crime! When I confront the client with this small complication, I always get, "But I didn't *sign* anything!" Ouch! Over the years I have developed the ability to not appear shocked or sickened or otherwise judgmental when the client tells me the vilest accounts of what he did, or what he is accused of doing. While my apparent nonchalance is good for the interviewing process, I often get concerned that I have become too insensitive as a human being, seeing that I can do this so well. What I have not been able to control in the last few years is my reaction to some aspect of the client's explanation that is either hysterically funny or very high up on the bullshit meter.

Not too long ago, a client came to see me with his "people" after he had been arrested for sexual assault. He was Albanian and spoke no English. I don't speak Albanian (see earlier reference to my poor academic record). He would speak a sentence or two in Albanian and his friend would translate it for me. It kind of went like this.

Client: *Nnclodf fnoei nsdhfo ldfo mdm.* (Well, that's what it sounded like to me . . .)

Friend: I met her at a bar and we went to my car.

Client: *Xnuio dhf do dojwer foi.*

Friend: We started kissing.

Client: *Lkskldk doifo dl blowjob.*

Friend: That is when she gave me a blow job.

Me: Wait a second—are you telling me that the Albanian word for "blow job" is . . . *blow job?* (I was shocked.)

Friend: *Cnkdj dlldjoi spieh blow job dloue blowjob?*

Client: *Soeij.*

Friend: Yes.

I spent the rest of the interview trying to not laugh. It was like when the nerdy kid in sixth grade gave an oral book report with his fly open! If I were to start recounting the incredible bullshit stories clients have shared with me over the years, we would need five more volumes of this book. My patience and bullshit tolerance have been stretched a bit too far. Sometimes I can't help myself, and I will respond to their tall tale with comments such as: "I give that story a three on a scale of one to ten. And you got two points for just writing the check." On the other hand, I have also learned not to dismiss a client's bullshit story so quickly. Occasionally, it ain't bullshit!

I once represented a man charged with possessing a lot of drugs and dealing the drugs with the assistance of his young teenage girlfriend. When he came in to see me after his arrest, he brought in the young girlfriend, who spun quite a story. My client had apparently set her up in a local motel room. When he was arrested, one of the officers picked her up at the motel for questioning. According to the girl, the officer took her to what he said was a "safe house," where he questioned her about my client's alleged drug dealing. She remembered the name on the mailbox of the home. Okay, so far I can buy this, kind of. But then her story got bizarre. She said she spent two nights with the officer at the house where the officer slept with her in the same bed! What really stuck out in her memory was the fact that there was this duck hanging over the bed, which was really weird. After a few days, according to the girl, the officer let her go. I personally knew this officer. There was no way in hell this could have happened. I thanked her for her help and told her we would certainly be calling her if and when we needed her .... NOT!

The case got pretty complicated, and it became necessary to have a preliminary hearing in front of a judge to determine whether the search, seizure, and arrest had been lawful. The credibility of the officers was essentially the focal point of the hearing. My client was a very nice guy who was incredibly knowledgeable about the law. One day during the hearing, I cited a case in my argument about some technical issue we were dealing with. My client then tapped me on the shoulder and reached into *his* briefcase and brought out LaFave's *Search & Seizure, Volume Three*. This is a legal research book that only the most experienced criminal defense lawyers have in their office. My client had all four volumes and had read and highlighted all the issues relevant to our case!

On a day off from the hearing, I was sitting in my office looking at my client's file and came across my notes from the young girlfriend. I called Information to find out if there was a telephone number for the name on the mailbox that she had given me. There was. I called the number and a lady answered. "Hello," I began. "My name is Mickey Sherman. I'm a local lawyer, and I apologize for taking up your time here, but I just wanted to ask you a question. It's kind of strange, but I hope you will bear with me for a moment."

"What would you like to know?" the woman on the other end asked suspiciously.

"Well, uh, by any chance, do you have a duck hanging over your bed?"

I'm now wondering how long it will take her to call the police on me.

"Absolutely not."

"Okay, thanks for—"

"It's a *mallard*! That is not just a duck! How do you know about it?"

Holy shit!

"Well, let me just ask you one more question. Do you know Officer Frank Thomas?"

"Of course I know him!" the woman exclaimed. "He's wonderful. He house-sits for me all the time. He's like a member of the family!"

"Well, was he 'house-sitting' for you on October seventeenth of this year?"

"Yes."

"Okay, one last question. Will you be around for the next few days, in case we need you in court?"

"Of course. I'm always willing to help Officer Thomas."

This girl was telling the truth! Who would have ever guessed that? Obviously not me. I subpoenaed the lady, the girl, and the officer. Proving that the officer may have engaged in some type of misconduct did not automatically exonerate my client, but it would be a very large problem for the State. When the officer and his chief showed up with lawyers, it was all over. The officer refused to testify, claiming his protection under the Fifth Amendment, which allowed him to not incriminate himself. My client went free, and they even had to give him back a boatload of cash they had seized from him.

Knowing that my client really did commit the crime for which he has been charged may be considered by some as an ethical burden, but I frankly believe it to be a luxury. I am in a much better position to know the strengths and weaknesses of the case and what chances I may have at trial. As stated earlier, I do get these clients—but not often. The vast majority of criminal clients fall into one of the following categories:

"Kind of Guilty" Clients, or "I Did It, but I Did It Because . . ." Clients

This group will tell me that they basically did what they are accused of doing, but they're really not guilty because they feel they have a valid defense:

A. He *did* have sex with the woman, *but* it was consensual.

B. He *did* give cocaine to the undercover agent, *but* he is not a dealer and was only sharing his stuff.

C. He *was* driving with an unlicensed illegal gun, *but* he needed it for self-defense because he handles a lot of cash in tough neighborhoods.

D. He *did* shoot, stab, punch, or kill the guy, *but* it was in self-defense.

E. He *did* forge his boss's name on the check, *but* they owed him the money.

Often these explanations fall far short of being legally valid defenses for the crimes committed; however, a decent explanation that is not too preposterous can often allow a jury to acquit, or perhaps prompt a prosecutor to use their discretion in reducing the charge or allowing a more palatable plea agreement. I once defended a young man for murder when he barged into another man's apartment, ran upstairs to the bathroom, and stabbed the victim to death while he was in the shower. The jury acquitted him after hearing that the victim had just given crack to my client's pregnant wife. In a somewhat exaggerated version of Nancy Reagan's "Just Say NO to Drugs!" campaign, my client had done what he needed to do to save the life and future of his wife and unborn child.

"Wait a Second . . . I Did Something—But Not That!" Clients

A.   He *did* mouth off to the cop, *but* didn't threaten to kill him and his family.

B.   He *did* steal cash from the gas station where he worked, *but* only a fraction of what the owner says is missing.

C.   He *did* have a fight with his wife, *but* he didn't grab her by the throat and stick her head in the toilet.

This is easily the most common explanation of why my client has been arrested. He did *something*, but not what he is accused of. The problem is that without a videotape of the incident, we *never* really know what truly happened. The victim has one story and the client has another. The police generally have a version, which has been related to them by either the victim or witnesses. Ironically, it has been proven over and over again that "eyewitness testimony" is often the lousiest and least trustworthy means to establish what really happened. Most players in the criminal justice system will agree that the truth is generally something in between the versions of the accused and the accuser. For example, one of my clients embezzled $4,000 from the petty-cash drawer at the gas station where he worked. Looking to cash in a bit more from his insurance company, the boss claimed my client stole ten times that amount!

I Didn't Do It! I Am Totally Innocent!

These are easily the most difficult clients to defend. There is no room for compromise or plea bargains. Either the charges are dismissed by means of various legal motions, or there is a trial. Along the way to this trial, both the defense and prosecution hope that the other side will blink. If the prosecutor senses that their case is a loser, they will either drop the charges or offer a plea bargain that is too good to refuse. Should the defense attorney realize that their case is hopeless, they will do their best to make the best deal possible, and then present it to the client as an alternative to a trial, the outcome of which is never a sure thing. This is where the problem lies. How do you tell your client he should strongly consider pleading *guilty* to a crime he has told you he did not commit?

When a client tells you he is innocent, he wants you to believe him. Quite logically, he neither appreciates nor accepts the proposition that a defense lawyer will try just as hard to win an acquittal for someone they believe is actually guilty. This, of course, is not supposed to be the case. In other words, the client believes that his lawyer has some inner voice in his gut telling him not to "get off" someone who really did it. Can you imagine? They actually attribute some real human qualities to us! When defense lawyers suggest the possibility of a guilty plea, it is often looked upon as a sign of "no confidence" in the client, his case, and perhaps even in *our own ability* to win the case. Often, this creates a rift in the relationship with the client that is very difficult to mend. Therefore, we rarely *know* for certain if our client is innocent or guilty. It is often a matter of how innocent he is or how guilty he is. That is why most of us never even try to guess in order to fill in the blanks. If a criminal lawyer has a problem with the issue of whether or not he knows for sure his client "did it" or "didn't do it," he should not be practicing criminal law. This issue should, simply put, not be an issue.

As I have said before, there have been occasions where I unquestionably *knew* my client was guilty. Not just "maybe guilty" or "probably guilty," but *absolutely guilty*—of murder.

Some twenty years ago, a very nice family came into my office with a serious problem. Tim Jones, my twenty-one-year-old client—a nice young man by all accounts—was joined by his parents. They told me that Tim had been apprehended while selling some property that had been owned by a man found murdered in his home that evening as he slept on his sofa. The police had arrested Tim, as well as his friend, Jay Benson, charging them with murder. However, their evidence was weak; they had no real forensic proof linking the suspects to the scene, other than the subsequent possession by both young men of some of the stolen items from the victim's home. Both young men insisted they were innocent, and that some other guy had given them the stolen property. Who was I to doubt their story? Tim had posted bail, but his "friend" Jay did not have the resources and was still sitting in jail. Tim's folks seemed like model parents and upstanding citizens of the community, and understandably, they wanted me to do everything I could to keep Tim from being wrongfully convicted of murder. They wrote me a decent-size check, and all three left the office.

Early the next morning, Tim came back to see me—alone. As he walked into the office, I felt a bit like a Gold Star Mother in World War II upon seeing a military car or a Western Union messenger pull up the long driveway to their Kansas farm. This was not going to be good news. In a rather matter-of-fact manner, Tim related to me that he had lied yesterday when his parents were with him. The real deal was this: Tim and his friend Jay had needed money for drugs. Jay knew that his landlord in Westport often kept a lot of cash around his apartment, and that it would be an easy score. Both boys broke into the man's home in the evening and stole his two portable TV sets, a calculator, and a car. They then went to another town and tried to sell the items. Tim explained that before they had broken into the apartment, neither of them had expressed any intention of killing the man, but when they walked in and saw him, Jay suddenly pulled out a gun and coolly shot his landlord in the head.

Tim told me that the two friends had spoken about the situation afterward, agreeing that if they kept their mouths shut, they would both walk away clean. Further, I was very specifically instructed by Tim not to share any of this information with anyone, including (and especially) his parents. *Uggghhh*. These people had come to me, asking me to do my best to protect their son. They had given me their hard-earned money, trusting that I would do the right thing for them. How could I *not* tell them what the real story was? How could I perpetuate Tim's lie? Sometimes this job sucks, and this was definitely one of those times. However, my marching orders clearly had to come from Tim and not his parents. I had to keep his confession to myself and sadly remain mute as he continued to lie to his parents.

What was my mission? Very simply, I needed to figure out what course of action would best protect Tim Jones, or at least minimize the penalties he might be facing. I asked him a great many questions about what had happened, and I wanted to know everything about his comrade, Jay, who was sitting in jail, not having had the money to post bail. I learned that Jay had lawyered up with a veteran criminal defense lawyer whom I knew quite well. He was a genuine character who greeted everyone with the salutation, "How's your sex life?" That silliness aside, he was very savvy, and I knew he would do anything to protect his client. I did agree with Tim that the evidence against him was not substantial, and that he did have a decent shot of toughing it out with a jury and *getting away with murder*. Could I do this as a lawyer? The answer is an unequivocal yes.

As I have said, I am not in the justice business. My job is to defend Tim. Ethically, my only restriction in defending him is not to promote or allow perjury. I am not supposed to make sure that "justice is done." I am there to get my client out of the courthouse with minimal consequences to his life. It is as simple as that.

It is fully within my job description to force the State to *prove* their case. What I cannot do is put Tim or anyone else on the witness stand when I believe they are going to lie about anything. I explained all this to Tim, and he was adamant that this was the road he wanted to go down. My problem here was not one of ethics, morality, conscience, or any other sentiment that would prevent me from assisting someone to be found "not guilty" for a murder in which he was involved. (Undoubtedly, this issue is what truly pisses most everyone off.) What bothered me was that I didn't think he/we would get away with it. His buddy Jay Benson was sitting in jail, with a clever lawyer who would size up the case the same way I was doing. This was going to be a race to the prosecutor's office. Whoever got there first and ratted out the other guy would get the best deal.

Tim told me this would never happen. He and Jay had a solemn pact not to screw one another over. They had discussed the evidence and knew that if they hung in there, they would both get off. I explained to Tim that I knew Jay's lawyer well, and that he would convince his client to make a deal. Moreover, my client had told me that Jay was the shooter, so we might be able to arrange a plea to a lesser charge and avoid the minimum twenty-five-year murder sentence if we stepped up to the plate now. Tim would not be persuaded. He wanted to roll the dice and go forward. I told him repeatedly that Jay and his lawyer would find a way to nail us. I emphasized that Jay was still in jail and must resent the fact that his partner was free on bond. The clanging of the jail bars has an effect on people that can lead them to rat out their own grandmother! Tim would still not be persuaded.

Several weeks later we appeared in court for our probable cause hearing. Also known as the "preliminary hearing," it is a kind of mini-trial wherein the State must show that probable cause exists, in order to continue the prosecution and place the accused on trial for the charge of murder. There are not many murders in the affluent and congenial town of Westport, Connecticut, so the courtroom was full. Sitting in the front row, right behind me, was my twelve-year-old son, Mark, who is now an accomplished lawyer, trying his own murder cases! He had never seen a murder trial and had come to watch his father in action. As we were about to begin the hearing, I realized that there were only two chairs at the defense table. Where were Jay Benson and his lawyer? I was told that they were waiving this hearing. This was not a good sign. Why couldn't I have gone into advertising like my mother had suggested?

The State put on a couple of police officers who described the scene, and the medical guy, who explained the cause of death. The prosecutor next began linking the murder to my client and his friend. He sought to prove that the young defendants were out that night trying to sell the television sets that were stolen from the victim's home after the man was shot to death. Their witness was a twenty-three year old character whom they pressured into testifying. He wasn't happy about being a prosecution witness and the transcript below certainly demonstrates that.

Direct Examination by the Prosecutor:

Q: *Do you recall January 25th of this year, Friday night?*
A: Well, now, that's what you said.

Q: *I'm asking if you recall that night?*
A: Well, now, that was a long time ago.

Q: *Do you recall being at the Dun-Rite Bar?*
A: I be at the bar and you said a certain date and I said yes, but I don't know if it was that exact date.

Q: *Did you tell me January 25th Friday night?*
A: Now, you say January 25th and I said, "Yeah," but I don't know if that was the exact date.

Q: *You want to change it a little bit now?*
A: I don't want to change nothin' now. Before I go on with all this, I would like to say something to you all, sir, just on my behalf from sitting in this chair, okay? Now, as I all said to you before, when I was downstairs, you can only believe half of what you hear and nothing of what you see. Now, I'm saying nothin' of

what you see and half of what you hear, so like even if I'm looking at this microphone it might be a gun, do you know what
I'm saying? And like I'm going to give you an example, now if
you have a mouse, a piece of cheese and a cat—

Prosecutor: Judge, I would ask that the witness be instructed to
answer the question.

A: Now, wait a minute. I'm appearing in this chair. This is a murder trial, do you know what I'm saying? And the other day you
told me I wasn't going to be implicated, you know what I'm
saying? And now I'm implicated.

The Court: Sir, you have a fifth amendment right not to make any
statement.

The Witness: Oh, I'm going to make a statement, Your Honor.

The Court: Any statement you may make may be used against you
so if you wish to take the fifth amendment, that's your right.

The Witness: No, I don't want to take the fifth. I want to stay with
a happy sixth.

The State then called someone who was a total stranger to me. My
description of what happened next cannot do justice to the
scene. The transcript says it best:

Direct Examination by the Prosecutor

Q: *Would you state your name?*

A: Louis A. Buonfiglio. (*This is his real name.*)

Q: *Would you state your occupation, sir?*

A: I'm a private investigator.

Q: *I want to draw your attention to February 22nd of this year; did you
have occasion to talk with Jay Benson [on that day]?*

A: Yes, I did.

Q: *At about what time was that?*

A: Approximately 7:22 in the evening.

Q: *And how did this conversation take place? What vehicle? Did you see him face-to-face, or in what fashion?*

A: Jay Benson called me from the Bridgeport Correctional Center at my office telephone.

Q: *And was this an agreed-upon situation?*

A: Yes, it was.

Q: *What type of setup was this, or arrangement?*

A: I advised him to call me at my home—at my office, rather. Between 7:00 and 8:00 P.M., because that was the time he was allowed to use the telephone from the Correctional Center, and in the course of that conversation he advised me, as he had in the past, relative to this particular crime, that he had nothing to do with it. He then advised me that—

MR. SHERMAN: *Sir, may we know the date again of this conversation? (A feeble attempt on my part to break up the flow here.)*

A: This was February 22nd.

Resumption of examination by the prosecutor:

Q: *And what type of phone do you have, sir?*

A: I have a total phone.

Q: *And while you had Jay Benson on the phone, what did you do?*

A: In agreement with Jay Benson, I then total-phoned him through to the home of Tim Jones, and Mr. Jones answered the phone.

Q: *And what, if anything, did you say to Tim Jones at that time?*

A: I just told him that we had a collect call from Jay to Tim, and would he accept, and he said he did.

Q: *And then what happened after that?*
A: I taped the conversation from that point on.

Q: *And did you hear what was said?*
A: Yes, I did.

At this point I objected to the tape being played, or being entered into evidence. I didn't know what was on it, but I knew it wasn't going to be good. The judge asked for the basis of my objection, and the transcript shows I claimed that it was in violation of the Constitution, the hearsay rule, the Fifth Amendment, and anything else I could think of. We even took a recess so I could grovel in the judge's chambers. In the end, the judge allowed the tape to be played.

The Tape

Mr. Buonfiglio: Hello. I have a collect call from Jay to Tim; will you accept, please?

Mr. Jones: Sure.

Mr. Buonfiglio: Okay, go ahead.

Mr. Benson: Hello.

Mr. Jones: (inaudible)

Mr. Benson: What's up, man?

Mr. Jones: (inaudible)

Mr. Benson: Were you sleeping?

Mr. Jones: Not anymore.

Mr. Benson: What?

Mr. Jones: Not anymore.

Mr. Benson: Did you just get up?

Mr. Jones: Yeah.

Mr. Benson: Could you talk a little bit louder? I can't hear you.

Mr. Jones: Yeah. What's going on?

Mr. Benson: I'm sorry. You know, Bridgeport. Wait a second. All right. Say it again.

Mr. Jones: I'm just trying to get my dollars right, man, read the Bible, and hope for this case to get over.

Mr. Benson: To get over, um? Hey listen, man—Monday, I'm going to go down and I'm going to give my statement, but, you know, Mary [their friend] and you—listen, I want an honest answer out of you, okay?

Mr. Jones: Yes.

Mr. Benson: You got to listen to this, man. This is very important. This is just for myself, you know, my personal sanity. I want to know—did you tell anyone else about you killing, you know, Lou, that night. I want to know because, you know, this is very important, because I don't want anything to backfire at my face.

Mr. Jones: Yeah. No, man, I ain't told nobody.

Mr. Benson: You didn't tell anybody else?

Mr. Jones: Unh-unh . . . outside the lawyer.

Mr. Benson: What?

Mr. Jones: Outside the lawyer.

Mr. Benson: Outside your lawyer? All right, you know, because—you didn't even tell Mary, right?

Mr. Jones: Unh-unh.

At this point, *everyone* in the courtroom was staring at me in disbelief, as if I'd grown another head on my shoulders. Their eyes said it all: HE KNEW! The lawyer *knew* his client did it, and he was going to let this guy get away with murder! I could see and feel their outraged thoughts, almost as if comic-book balloons filled with angry words had appeared above their heads. I looked at my son in the first row. How was I going to explain this to him? Would he understand that this was my job—that it was my *obligation* to defend someone, even if I actually knew he had committed the crime? Trying to make believe that this evidence was not really so damning, I sat there taking notes as the tape played on. Jay asked a couple of questions about their friend Mary, and then finished the conversation by very cleverly date-stamping the conversation:

Mr. Benson: All right, listen, man. All right, let's keep the faith, okay? Don't worry about me. You know, and just do your thing, okay, and I'll see you Tuesday. If there's any messages to give Mary, just let me know, okay?

Mr. Jones: Yeah.

Mr. Benson: Just keep the faith, man, and I'll talk to you later, okay?

Mr. Jones: All right.

Mr. Benson: Hey, you know, is it January? What's the date today?

Mr. Jones: Today is the 23rd.

Mr. Benson: The 22nd?

Mr. Jones: The 22nd.

Mr. Benson: Man, it's been a long time since I've been here.

Mr. Jones: I know.

Mr. Benson: I know it. So, I know it, like I know that you and Mary have been trying to get me out, man, but I certainly get upset, really, because, you know, because I tell you, I, you know, your and Mary's help, you know. It doesn't make any sense to spend all that money to get me out, whereas my lawyer feels, you know (inaudible) the case.

Mr. Jones: Oh yeah?

Mr. Benson: Yeah, so listen, I appreciate the effort, though, and I don't think—

Mr. Jones: Well, we'll both walk it until it's safe, man.

Mr. Benson: Yeah, I know. Listen man, do you think, you know, keep the faith and I'll talk to you.

Not long after that hearing, I was able to arrange a plea whereby Tim received a sentence of thirty years, five more than the minimum, yet thirty-five less than the maximum. Jay got thirty *months*! He had been successful in both netting Tim *and* convincing the prosecutor and judge that he was not the shooter. Eighteen years later, I got a letter from Tim, written from prison.

Dear Mickey Sherman:
Many years have passed since we last communicated. I am contacting you for two reasons. The first is something I wanted to do for a long time. That is to extend my sincere apology for not being straightforward as well as truthful with you and my family in this case you settled for us. I was not

innocent at all, as you may have suspected. Shortly after coming to prison I told my parents I committed that murder. Unlike today, in 1985 I was too ignorant and full of myself to be straightforward with anyone. Because of that I got what I deserved. After everything was over, I realized the erroneousness of that attitude towards those who were trying to help me. Again I apologize to you for that.

In 2007, while preparing for the publication of this book, I dropped a note to my client who was still in prison. I wanted to make sure it was OK with him to publish his letter above. His response bears reproducing here as well:

I am doing very well Mickey, thank you. How are you these days....I have been working, attending college and for the most part setting my life back on track....Over the years I have participated in social programs designed for straight talk group sessions where inmates tell their stories to high school and middle school youths. We also worked extensively with at risk youths in the Alternative to Incarceration Centers and Day Incarcerations Centers.

He wished me well with the book and added, *"However I may positively contribute to this endeavor, by all means utilize the letter."*

I have never been a big believer in the success of our corrections department in actually *rehabilitating* people. These letters strongly suggest I may very well be wrong about that. My client has totally "gotten it" and seems to be ready to get out of prison soon and become a very useful member of society.

In short, he did it. I knew he did it. He paid his price for doing it and now is ready for a second chance at life. That is kind of the way the system is supposed to work.

So . . . I *can* represent someone when I *know* they are guilty. I will generally do my best to find another avenue for the client other than a trial, and I know that if it does ultimately go to trial, it might very well end in disaster. Yet, I do not have a problem with this basic issue. For some reason, however, *everyone else* has a problem with it, and that is why we are always greeted with the same ol', same ol'—"So how can you defend . . ."

Sometimes the greeting is a bit less kind. I was recently on a flight from L.A. to New York City when a flight attendant began asking me about various big cases in the news. She then told me how she had met the late Johnnie Cochran on one of her flights. She was following a little older woman down the aisle who walked by Cochran while he was reading a book, minding his own business. Instead of a hello or some other greeting, she loudly proclaimed, "SHAME ON YOU, JOHNNIE COCHRAN!" without breaking stride. As Hyman Roth told Michael Corleone in *The Godfather: Part II*, "This is the business we've chosen."

{Chapter 3}

Aren't You Afraid to
Deal with "*Those People*"?

WHO ARE "*THOSE PEOPLE*"? Until their son, uncle, dentist, or stock-broker gets arrested for something, most people assume that the people who get arrested are low-life degenerates who spend their days stealing from us and their evenings having sex with animals and downloading child pornography on the Internet. This hardly describes Martha Stewart, Kobe Bryant, Robert Blake, or your brother-in-law. In truth, almost anyone can find his or her way into the criminal justice system. Those folks who have been unlucky enough to get arrested come from all walks of life and should not be painted with the broad brush of being some kind of *untermenschen*!

But the Ivy League pedigree of your client does not mean they are going to be easy to deal with; often, the reverse is true. Most criminal defense lawyers will tell you that they would much rather represent a career criminal or a guy from the street than a dot-com, hedge-fund yuppie with a big bank account. This is true for any number of reasons. The street guy has been through this process before. He knows that I am his only shot of staying out of jail, or at least minimizing his time. Regardless of his formal education, he is probably "court-wise" and knows he should tell me the straight story so we don't get surprised or sandbagged later on in the case. He may not be proud of his actions, but is generally not too embarrassed to tell me the whole story.

An interesting fact about the street criminal concerns who actually hires me. The hedge-fund guy, if he is locked up, sends his family, friends, or his real lawyer to meet with me, hire me, and pay me if they decide I am the one they want. The street guy sends his "people." His people may be relatives, but I often never get the real picture of who they are. It isn't really important, other than the fact that I must satisfy myself that they are not paying me with drug money or money that has been stolen from the victim in the case at hand (or maybe from another victim of a previous crime).

Quoting and charging legal fees to rich clients is often an interesting experience. Every seasoned criminal defense lawyer knows that you have to quote and collect the fee *up front*. I often say that this exercise must be done while the client is still "in the SOUP." (You have to get them to write the check while they are still feeling the Sense Of Urgency and Panic!) I am not making the case for taking advantage of people while they are behind the eight ball. It is just a fact of life that the prospective client values the lawyer's services a lot more immediately following the arrest process. He or she has had a taste of the humiliation and pain of having been arrested. This "appreciation" of my worth to him will only last so long. If I don't get him to actually write that check immediately, I might be in trouble, as the status of my accounts receivable will be very far down on his list of priorities in the weeks and months to come.

How do we set fees? Most "real" lawyers charge by the hour. They bill the clients for their faxes, mailings, e-mails, lunches, telephone calls, and God only knows what else. Criminal lawyers generally do not follow this model. We tend to charge a flat fee. Most often the criminal lawyer will ask for a retainer for all his efforts up to trial, and then another fee for going to trial. I usually charge just one fee. It covers everything: phone calls, court appearances, hearings, motions, and a trial if one is called for. I have found that clients would rather pay a lot of money right up front and know that this is the whole deal, rather than be surprised as the bill keeps getting bigger. The proliferation of lawyer jokes is proof positive that we are not the most trusted group of people in society. Clients are skeptical of our charging them so much money per hour while we bullshit in the courthouse hallways with our friends, all on the client's dime. I try and take this fear off the table by telling the client that if I want to delay the case or come back to court another day to shop for a different judge, it is not costing them a penny more. I also like the idea of allowing people to decide to go to trial without factoring in a large extra fee.

The only problem is explaining to the client that I need the fee *now*. Most people do appreciate this, but some cannot fathom the idea of paying for something they have not yet received. One prospective client was clearly a savvy businessman who wanted me to tell him that I would basically guarantee he would "get off." I gave him my standard promise: "I will show up and do my best." He asked me what my fee was.

"Seventy-five hundred dollars," I calmly replied.

"Well, Mr. Sherman," he whined, "suppose I don't like the result of the case. Will you still expect me to pay you seventy-five hundred dollars?"

"No," I quickly responded. "Because if you hire me, I want the seventy-five hundred up front. You will have already paid me!"

He was incredulous. "You mean, you expect me to pay you the entire fee up front?"

"Yup."

"Well, let me tell you something. I am in the service business myself, and I don't ask for all the money up front. In fact, sometimes I don't get paid all the money even after I perform the service!"

"Exactly!" I said. He was a perfect expert witness for my cause here. I couldn't resist rubbing it in. "That's why I ask for all the money up front. And there's no extra charge for this business lesson!" He kind of stormed out of the office, but came back the next day—with $7,500. Over the years he has referred many clients to me.

Quoting and collecting fees from clients is often not what people might expect. As mentioned above, the street criminal or habitual offender is probably the easiest person to deal with in terms of fees. Drug dealers and other clients who regularly steal sometimes keep a stash in a bank or in their sock drawer for the lawyer when they get busted. They know they will need it, and for them, it's just the cost of doing business. Organized crime clients are likewise very easy to deal with when it comes to fees. They understand that the lawyer needs to get paid up front. All they generally demand is that we do our best, pay attention to every detail of their case, and don't bullshit them. That is not a lot to ask. They also know what is realistic and appreciate that we are not magicians. Unlike the hedge-fund guy, they don't expect us to deliver an apology from the prosecutor on the first court date.

There are certain clients who require very special skills in the fee-quoting and -collecting session, and one category is gypsies. That's right, gypsies. Almost every year, a crew of gypsies manages to find their way to affluent communities like Greenwich, Connecticut. Usually it's women. One will knock on the front door, asking for some water for her young child, who is either in her arms or in a nearby car. While the homeowner (or their nanny) is getting them the water or milk, another woman has slipped in the back door and is emptying all the jewelry from the upstairs bedroom into a pillowcase that has been quickly removed from the bed. Within minutes, they are on their way. They get nabbed when they do more than one house in the neighborhood and the police close in. They are arrested and kept in jail. They may make bond if it is not too outrageous, but as often as not, they are kept in jail to go to court the next day.

That is when I get visited by the King of the Gypsies. I am not making this up. Somebody named Joe or Nick will come to my office with one or more of his associates, who never open their mouths. The King tells me that, first, he is "The King," and some of his people have been unjustifiably arrested and wrongfully charged with burglary when they were just asking some homeowner for directions to God knows where.

"What are their names?" I ask. "Do they have records? Will they come back to court if I can convince the judge to let them out on bail?" I ask these questions out of some sense of obligation. In truth, I am not going to get anything that remotely resembles the truth. But like a nine-year-old Jewish kid at Passover, I have to go through the asking of the four questions. (Gentile readers, please Google "Passover" + "Four Questions" to appreciate this metaphor.)

The names of the clients are always a trip. The police have arrested them under one name and the King is telling me their names are totally different. Why is this? I never get a straight answer, other than the cops screwed up. Neither name seems to ever have any vowels in it. (Seinfeld makes the same comment about New York City taxi drivers, but I don't think there is any connection.) The King tells me that they have never been arrested before and their passports are in the back of somebody's car whose dog ate their homework. They need to get out on bail because they are suffering from some disease that can't really be named, but they really need to get out of jail.

Now if I know this stuff, the prosecutor and judge know the drill as well. I am being hired to convince the prosecutor and judge to let them plead guilty to something and pay a really big fine. They cannot be on probation because they . . . well, they have to get to Palm Beach or Shaker Heights to do their thing. Luckily enough for them, the prose- cutor and judge don't want them on probation here because that means they will be staying longer in our community and other people's homes will be at risk. Let them move on. Hit them with a big fine or let them out on bail that is large enough to justify their skipping out.

The King and I are on the same page. I know what he wants, and I tell him if I think I can do it or not. If I don't think I can help, I don't want to get involved. Generally, I think I can help, and that is when the game show begins. The King tells me that he has heard all about me and the incredible talents I have in helping people, and how he knows

I am going to do a great job for him and his people, and that they (his people) will be sending me many, many clients who have been similarly screwed by the police, and I will become very wealthy as a result of their having anointed me as "house counsel" to this sect of gypsies.

Yeah, yeah, yeah . . . thanks so much, that is terrific, but let's get on with it. The *it* is how much I want to take this case right now. Both the King and I know that the guy to his right (who has not uttered a word but often nods in agreement) has a brown bag in his jacket with cash in it. My job is to figure out how much is in that bag. What is their *budget*? I start high, they chisel me down. I come down, they inch up a bit. We both get insulted and they leave, only to come back. I throw them out of the office a couple of times. About eighty minutes later, we have agreed on the fee and the bag comes out. My heart races as I watch the money come out of the bag. The nightmare is that they were prepared to spend a lot more money than I charged them and fistfuls of bills are still sitting in their bag after they pay me my fee! In the last few years I have lost a lot of my patience with this process. It has ceased to be as much fun as it used to be. Maybe it is a sign that I need to get into a different line of work.

What I do now is abbreviate the process. In a tone not unlike Alex Trebek announcing the rules for Final Jeopardy, I go with, "Okay, King, why don't we just do this. I asked for ten thousand. You and your friend got pissed off and walked out. I then followed you out and you came back with five thousand. I then told you how insulted I was, and so forth and so on. Let's just make believe it is about an hour from now and we have agreed on seven thousand dollars, and that's that. We both have an extra hour and a half or so to enjoy our lives instead of having wasted it doing this shtick." Believe it or not, this generally works. I know that a lot of people will think that I am making this stuff up. I'm not. I guess I might piss off a lot of gypsies by having related this information here, but hopefully they will have already bought the book on Amazon.

When charging fees, the criminal defense lawyer has to make sure he is not being paid with dirty money. It is our responsibility to do our best to learn that we are not being paid with money that has been stolen from someone else. Likewise, we are on thin ice if we accept money that we have good reason to believe has been earned by some illicit behavior by the client. When a drug dealer comes in with bundles of twenties, that's an easy call. But when someone is charged with embezzling money from their employer, should we be skeptical about taking a check from them, drawn on their personal account? There are a couple of real problems with this issue. First, how effective a detective does the lawyer want to be, knowing that if he does too good a job in investigating the prospective client's sources of income, he may feel compelled to turn the client away, passing up a sweet payday? The dilemma is obvious. The more information we get, the less likely it might be that we will get paid.

Some lawyers basically mimic the airline clerk who asks us if anyone else packed our luggage or gave us anything to carry. Our version is, "Hey, you didn't steal this money from anyone, did you?" After a "No," or even a slight shaking of the head, our forensic accounting work is done. This can be very problematic a bit down the road, however. Should the prosecution track the proceeds of the client's crimes, the lawyer may, at the very least, be obligated to turn over the money given to him. At worst, we might be subject to some form of prosecution. This is remote but certainly not worth the risk. The safer path is to really make a reasonable inquiry into the source of the funds.

I once represented a very nice lady who had embezzled several hundred thousand dollars from a local company. She had a boatload of money in her personal account, located at a bank just a block away from my office. She told me that some of the money wasn't stolen but was part of her savings. Did I believe her? I sure wanted to. I resolved the issue by calling the United States Attorney's office (with her knowledge and consent) and telling the prosecutor assigned to the case where the money was, and how much was there. I asked him directly if he had a problem with my client giving me a check for my fee from that account, which also clearly contained stolen funds. I told him how much the fee would be and he felt it was reasonable. He gave me the okay, and I got paid. This issue is generally not that easy to resolve. The criminal defense lawyer often has to make a tough call. It is one of the land mines of the profession.

There is another element involved, which does not help the exercise of asking clients for money. We, the defense lawyers, are often looked upon by the client as just one more cog in the big horrible machine that is grinding the life and happiness out of him. He got arrested by *the cops*. He is brought to the police station or the court, where he has to pay a lot of money to *the bail bondsman*. He then goes in front of *the judge*, where he hears a lot of crappy stuff being said about him in public by *the prosecutor*. And then, he has to write a big check, his hard-earned money, to . . . *the LAWYER!* We are just one of the players making his life miserable in this hell he finds himself in.

Very often, I see former clients out in the real world, at a restaurant or charity benefit or whatever. They will see me and turn away quickly so as not to have to say hello. I totally understand this. It has nothing to do with my egomaniacal personality, or his seeming lack of appreciation for my having done a good job for him. It is very simple: I remind him of a very unpleasant chapter in his life. Why should he have to be reminded of it, or be obliged to explain to his friends how he knows me? The yuppie, executive, or celebrity is often very embarrassed to tell me exactly what happened, so he will shade his version of the incident so he doesn't look like too much of a schmuck. He is overly concerned about how he will be judged by his family, his coworkers, his friends, and even his lawyer. This is a great handicap.

On one occasion, I was the one who avoided making eye contact with a former client. I was hired to represent a commercial airline pilot who had been arrested for threatening his wife and child with a gun. He was a longtime captain with a major airline and had a very unusual name. For the purposes of this book, we will call him Captain Wolfsberg. He had held his wife and child hostage for hours and threatened to blow his own brains out several times. The police handled the situation quite well, and Wolfsberg surrendered without anyone being hurt. Obviously he had some serious psychiatric problems, and his defense consisted of his being committed to an institution for a few months, after which he followed up with intensive psychiatric treatment.

About four or five months after the trial, I was on a plane with my family, taxiing down the runway, about to take off from Bermuda. After the flight attendants enlightened us on how to buckle and unbuckle the seatbelt, the following announcement came over the loudspeaker:

"Hello, this is Captain Wolfsberg and I expect an easy flight to New York . . . ."

Holy shit! This was my client. I knew which airline he had worked for, and how many Captain Wolfsbergs could there be? The entire flight, I never got out of my seat. I had convinced myself that if he saw me he would have a flashback and God knows what would happen. I did run into him years later and actually told him the story. He laughed and assured me he was fine then and is fine now.

I once represented a lawyer for drunk driving. He had flipped his car over and was standing near the overturned vehicle when the police came upon him. He told me he hadn't had too much to drink, and this was really a bogus charge by a rookie cop who had an attitude. He demanded a trial. The police reports were more or less routine. DWI reports are always identical. I am convinced that there is some special key on the cops' typewriters which, when touched lightly, churns out the same crap for each arrest:

When asked for his license and registration, the operator fumbled though his glove compartment and had difficulty finding his license in his wallet. He had a strong odor of alcohol on his breath and was wobbling and swaying . . .

. . . and so forth and so on. I am convinced that if a police officer from anywhere in this country ever stopped the pope, the report would read the same.

As this lawyer's trial date neared, I went to see the young cop, just to get a feel for how he would do on the stand when I embarrassed the hell out of him with my brilliant cross-examination. He told me he was glad to have the chance to talk to me because he had left a few things out of his report. *Great!* This hotshot had screwed up, and was actually going to share with me how sloppy his investigation was. He proceeded to tell me that my client was *not* near the car when the officer had found him. He was *on top* of the car, urinating onto the smoking tire. He had already defecated in his pants but waited to vomit all over himself until he was in the back of the police car. The young officer did not put this into his report because he knew the guy was a local lawyer and didn't want him to be embarrassed at court. Later, I confronted my client with this version. It was totally true. We never went to trial.

When famed sportscaster Marv Albert was facing charges of sexually assaulting a woman, he steadfastly maintained his innocence, refusing any plea bargain. The incident was a bizarre one, and his attorney, Roy Black, had great information to work with relative to the history of Albert and his accuser. As they proceeded toward trial, more "victims/ partners" came out of the woodwork to accuse Albert of other bizarre conduct. They cut a deal that worked out nicely. Now, Roy Black is one of the best in the business; why didn't he cut the deal earlier? Why did he wait until his client was totally embarrassed by all the silly crap that was regurgitated nightly on TV? My theory: Albert never told his lawyer about the other stuff. He is a world-class broadcaster and didn't want to embarrass himself by telling his lawyer about dressing up in women's underwear, and so on. Understandable—but not helpful to his case.

In the end, Roy Black did a great job, and Albert conducted himself very appropriately; he was contrite, remorseful, and pretty classy, given the circumstances. He made it through the "system," and eventually back to the top of the broadcasting world. We love to watch our celebrities stumble, fall, and embarrass themselves. But, thankfully, we also like to watch them climb out of their hellhole and get back on top.

Unless they act like a total schmuck *all* the time, we seem to like to forgive people who screw up. That has to be a good thing.

The arrest process often has a very humbling effect on people, irrespective of their affluence, position, or status as a celebrity. Granted, there are some celebrities who just cannot or will not change their manner to suck up to the criminal justice machinery. No better example of this attitude or ignorance can be found than the famous Michael Jackson display, when he danced on the roof of his SUV outside the courthouse after showing up twenty minutes late for his arraignment. The Jackson show was an exception. While he is a brilliant entertainer and musical genius, he appeared to demonstrate total contempt for the criminal justice process and the players therein, especially the judge. You don't always have to kiss up to the judge, but it's generally not a good idea to publicly give him the finger, which was the essence of Jackson's SUV moonwalk.

Michael Jackson notwithstanding, the rich and powerful are usually humbled by the arrest process. They have been humiliated and shamed by their arrest, and the publicity and notoriety that often go along with it. They often possess substantial egos and feel that everyone on the planet has seen the headline, page-three story, or just the blurb in the local police blotter reporting their arrest. A psychiatrist might call this a "narcissistic wound." Their feeling of self-importance unreasonably magnifies their humiliation. For the criminal lawyer, this is a good thing. While this "upper demo" client (really, really rich and powerful) is generally accustomed to ordering around his lawyers, accountants, brokers, and so forth, that dynamic disappears after the arrest. He is generally all too aware that his fate is in my hands. He is transformed into a very docile, manageable person who will jump through any hoops I suggest.

We saw this classic humble behavior on the part of NBA basketball superstar Kobe Bryant during the entire episode of his Colorado rape case. He *never* strutted around or acted in an offensive manner at any time. He would routinely open the car door for his attorney and appeared to be a perfect gentleman at all times, apparently devoid of the demons that we had been led to believe caused him to brutalize his victim. I complimented his attorney, Pam Mackey, on the great job she did in coaching him to behave so humbly during the case. She told me that she hadn't done any coaching; he was just that kind of guy. I believe her. I have learned that some people are too often incapable of being coached or taking such direction, which made Bryant's behavior even more impressive.

Years ago I represented the great actor George C. Scott not long after he won the Academy Award for *Patton*. He was involved in a dispute in Greenwich and was arrested for a fairly minor offense after a verbal argument about the World Series. When he came to see me, I was prepared to meet an arrogant, swaggering General Patton. I was sure he was going to either slap me or holler at me. Nothing could have been further from what actually transpired. He told me the whole story, blemishes and all. He was ready to do anything or say anything I suggested to cooperate in his defense. He could not have been easier to deal with in every respect. This surely was the "humbling" effect at work.

I may have actually gone a bit too far in dealing with Scott and his amiability back then. The prosecutors agreed to dismiss all the charges. I was running from one court to another that day and didn't have a chance to tell him the good news. As we were about to walk into the courtroom to make the case go away, he very nervously said, "Mickey . . . What's going to happen? What are you going to say?" I quickly replied, "Me? I'm not sayin' anything. You have to do the talking. Didn't you see you in *Anatomy of a Murder*? You were brilliant!" As he stared at me, speechless, I walked in and sat with the other lawyers waiting for the case to be called. Luckily, he thought it was pretty funny too, once it was all over.

Dealing with the criminal client is not something that all lawyers can do. For some reason, there are criminal lawyers who seem to get annoyed and angry when their clients get into trouble. I can never understand this. They're *supposed* to get in trouble. That is why they are called "clients." If they didn't screw up, we would have to do regular, boring lawyer stuff! Because it's more likely than not that our clients will get in trouble again, it is our responsibility to factor that in when determining how to deal with someone's case. For example, someone with several convictions for shoplifting obviously has a problem. What I would not want to do is make a plea bargain that would put that person on probation for an extended time with a substantial suspended jail sentence. We are just setting the client up for a long jail sentence within a short period of time when they get arrested again, which is a virtual certainty. What I want to do with this person is have them pay a large fine instead of probation.

Most states have some type of pretrial diversionary programs, which allow people to be treated leniently on their first arrest. Often, however, these are "get out of jail free" cards, which can only be used once. Thus, we have to look at the client and figure out if we should use it now or save it for their next crime! I never have a problem explaining this to clients. You would expect they would be insulted that I am assuming they will screw up again, but more often than not, they appreciate my thinking that far ahead.

It does take a fair amount of patience to deal with clients at times. There is often some chromosome imbalance or something that allows them to think (or not think) a bit differently than most other people. It is not exactly like thinking "outside the box." It is more absurd than that. Often, they seem to make perfectly good sense, and all of the sudden, you find yourself on Mars. A couple of examples:

I represented a young man who had been arrested with his friends for stealing a car and going on a joyride. He candidly told me that *he* had stolen the car and told his friends it belonged to his cousin; his pals had absolutely no idea the vehicle was stolen. When we went to court, the lawyers for the friends asked me if my client would admit this to the prosecutor and "cut them loose." This made sense to me. He would get credit for his honesty, and aside from the strategic issue, it was the right thing to do. These other kids were innocent. I asked my client's father if it was okay for me to let the prosecutor know that the other kids had had no knowledge of the crime.

"NO WAY!" screamed the father. "Why should the other kids get off?"

"Well . . . they didn't do anything wrong," I calmly explained.

The father thought for a moment and then came up with a classic. "Well, aren't they still responsible because of guilt by association?"

"Uhhh . . . gee . . . I never thought of that angle," I said (still trying to reason with him), "but guilt by association is a *bad thing*, not a legal principle." It fell on deaf ears. The father was too pissed off that his kid had screwed up. I asked the kid if I could tell the prosecutor the truth. To his credit, he readily agreed.

Sometimes clients can be *too* honest. True story: A husband and wife got arrested for dealing cocaine out of their home. They contacted me to represent them. It is generally not a good idea for one lawyer to represent more than one person in a criminal prosecution. Too often, one is more or less guilty than the other, and the prosecution may want you to trade one client for another in some fashion. Your lawyer should be just that: *your* lawyer. There should be no diluting of his loyalty to you in the case. So when this couple called, I had to decide which one to represent, and which one to refer to a friend. All things considered, it's best to send the guiltier one to another lawyer! Eventually we worked out a deal where the wife was pleading guilty to a misdemeanor and the husband was getting a short jail term. As we stood before the judge, our clients were entering their pleas of guilty and being "canvassed." The judge asked them a series of questions to make sure that they were, in fact, admitting to this crime, and that they were aware of their rights. The other lawyer and I stood there, somewhat bored by this procedure, as we had heard it about seven thousand times. Finally, the prosecutor recited what the husband's conduct had been. "Mr. Katz sold a certain amount of cocaine, which, upon testing, was found to be seventy-five percent pure—"

"That's a lie!" shouted the husband, interrupting the prosecutor.

The judge jerked his head up and the entire courtroom became still. It is common for the client to disagree with the prosecutor's reciting of the facts of the crime. They often have an overexaggerated version, which was given to them by the police or the victim. My friend tried to quiet him down before the judge held him in contempt or the deal was blown.

"No! I'm sorry . . . I got a reputation in this town! I wouldn't sell crap like that. My stuff is *pure*! That stuff was ROCK!" (Whatever that means . . .)

My co-counsel and I totally expected to hear protestations of how the police had overexaggerated the quality and value of the drugs. As mentioned above, that is the nature of the game. We *never* anticipated the client would be so outraged that the police and court were questioning the *quality* of the cocaine he was selling. This was a first for all of us.

We all stood there in disbelief—the judge, the defense lawyers, and the prosecutor. None of us knew what to do. We finally postponed the case for a month until the husband agreed to plead guilty and also suffer a professional insult as a drug dealer.

A sense of humor is often a very necessary tool for all of us in the criminal justice world. Cops are no exception. I know a judge who was once arrested for a domestic disturbance with his wife. When the police got to his home, they quieted things down and asked him the routine question: "Do you have a gun in the house?" His reply was priceless. "No—can I borrow yours!" Luckily for this judge, those cops did have a sense of humor.

Without a doubt, many people consider the defense lawyer to be some kind of "partner in crime" with our clients. They choose to confuse our vigor in defending them *after* they have committed some crime with some motivation on our part to *help* or encourage them to commit crimes. If our client doesn't show up in court, it's the lawyer who gets hollered at!

Some years ago, I represented a young man who did not show up in court for the trial of two cases of sexual assault. The case received a great deal of media attention and was the subject of at least one book and TV movie. My client, Alex Kelly, was missing for nine years before he turned himself in to authorities. For the first six months of his disappearance, I was not only constantly questioned by the FBI's Fugitive from Justice unit, but was actually followed by a bounty hunter who sought the reward being offered for his capture. This guy did not exactly "blend" into the crowd. I finally dealt with it by making sure I introduced him to anyone I was with at each encounter. "Hi—just want you to meet Frank the Bounty Hunter here who kind of follows me around everywhere." The first time I did he was really pissed off. After a couple of months, he not only enjoyed the introduction but would usually send drinks to my table as a thank-you for making him just a tiny bit famous.

A common misconception is that a defense lawyer is the natural enemy of prosecutors and the police. This is simply not the case. We kind of all work at the same factory. Of course, we have different roles and objectives, but we deal in the same commodity, suffer the same problems with the system, and speak the same language. People outside the system don't get our jokes, and generally lump us all together as those annoying people who make them show up for jury duty.

The great majority of police officers have absolutely no ill feelings toward defense lawyers. They understand and appreciate our role, and do not take it personally when we try to decapitate them on the witness stand. As long as we don't take cheap shots or lie, they harbor no grudges. Police officers often refer clients to us, since they have seen us in the pit. They know who is a great lawyer in the coffee shop but cannot try a case in court. We criminal lawyers routinely get clients referred to us by police officers with whom we've locked horns in the courtroom. Likewise, prosecutors are often our close friends. It is quite common for us to almost come to blows in court and then go to lunch together to talk about what idiots our coworkers are.

This can be a problem that most lawyers do not appreciate. A few years ago I was one of the lecturers in a legal seminar out west somewhere. The speaker who preceded me was Susan McDougal, the unfortunate target of Ken Starr's prosecutorial zeal in his campaign to nail the Clintons. She had refused to testify against anyone, and maintained that the government wanted her to perjure herself. She wound up spending some serious time in jail for contempt and was put on trial several times. During one of her trials, she had been represented by Mark Geragos (before he represented Scott Peterson). She spoke of how wonderful Geragos was to her and how well he had represented her, but she was disconcerted by one thing: He would often chat with the prosecutors during recesses, and appeared to be quite amiable with them. One of the prosecutors asked him if he could help his daughter get a job somewhere, and Geragos gave the prosecutor his home number. *So where is the problem here?* I thought to myself as McDougal went on.

"Those bastards were trying to put me in jail—and my lawyer was being nice to them, right in front of me!" Susan McDougal said. She told us about how she had pulled Geragos aside, telling him how pissed off she was at this. Geragos explained to her the essential structure that I have outlined above. He assured her that it is his nature to be friendly, and that he would still be fighting hard in court. She didn't care. They were the enemy, and she resented his apparent collaborative behavior.

I found this complaint of hers to be not only fascinating but also very illuminating. Being the same kind of schmoozer as Geragos, it had never occurred to me that my clients might feel some sort of betrayal by my friendly behavior. This was not the first time I had heard such a complaint. Often, clients of the public defender would complain that their lawyers must be selling them out because they saw them "all go to lunch together." I had always assumed that my clients probably thought it was a *good* thing that I was tight with the prosecutors. I didn't think they believed the prosecutors were going to lay down for me in the case. But common sense would dictate that we would be less likely to be blindsided or screwed by a prosecutor with whom I was friendly. Susan McDougal showed me that I was wrong. The unfortunate citizen who has become the target of the prosecution does *not* want to see us fraternizing and joking with the very person who is the architect of his destruction. It is not at all important that the client's take on this relationship is wrong. What is important is how our behavior affects our client's *perception* of our allegiance to them.

I have done my best to remember this lesson since I heard McDougal's lecture—and not always with success. During the trial of Michael Skakel, I went to lunch one afternoon with Henry Schlief, CEO of Court TV. Henry is a friend, and we often play golf together. This was not a media interview. Henry had invited Dominick Dunne to join us in his limousine as we returned to the courthouse after lunch. Dominick had written article after article in *Vanity Fair* magazine, condemning my client and, depending on the month, me as well. He had written two books dealing with the case and had appeared on many television shows, declaring my client's guilt. I had known Dominick Dunne for several years before the Skakel case, and we did our best to remain friendly by basically not talking about the case. An uneasy yet effective truce.

Apparently, when we pulled up to the courthouse, members of my client's family saw me get out of the limousine with Dominick Dunne. They were, and probably continue to be, incensed with me about that. I could have explained to them that Dunne, opinionated as he may have been about the case, had shared some information with me over the last few years, which had actually been very helpful to the defense. As Don Corleone taught us all, "Keep your friends close, and your enemies closer." In retrospect, I believe this would not have made them feel any less betrayed. They were right—and I was wrong. I had forgotten Susan McDougal's lesson: Regardless of my intentions, the mere *appearance* of hanging out with the enemy was totally offensive to my client's family.

I have tried to make a conscious effort *not* to be so chummy with prosecutors in the presence of my clients, but I know I am not that successful. It is my nature to shmooze and kid with people, and I generally cannot help myself.

{Chapter 4}

Are
There Cases or
Clients That
You Won't Take?

ONE OF THE ADVANTAGES of being a private criminal defense lawyer is that you don't have to take everyone's case. I am frequently asked what cases I turn down. For some reason, everyone expects me to say that I won't represent clients if I know or believe they may be guilty. There is a word for lawyers who go by that standard; they are called "poor." There are exceptions to my observation, but very few. In fact, I am pretty sure there is only one: Barry Sheck. Having established the Innocence Project in New York and elsewhere, he has been responsible for the often very late and heart-wrenching correction of some incredible miscarriages of justice throughout the country. He has earned the right to draw such a difficult line in the sand in our profession.

So how can the rest of us actually champion the cases of clients we believe to be guilty? There is a substantial percentage of the population that believes we are as evil, or perhaps more evil, than our clients for not letting this question bother us. They chalk it up to some rationalization on our part to make money by prostituting our sense of values. It is kind of like a permutation of one of my favorite lawyer jokes:

Question: How much is two and two?
Lawyer: How much do you need it to be?

Our perception, guess, or actual knowledge of our client's guilt is generally a nonissue. How can this be? Shocking as it may sound, we generally believe everyone who hires us is probably guilty of something. That's why they need us! Their apparent guilt is hardly ever a factor in determining whether we want to represent them or not. As was discussed in the first chapter of this book, we are often not the best judges of our client's guilt or innocence, and we have no business setting ourselves up as their judge and jury. Our job is to defend them within the bounds of the law and rules of the court. End of discussion.

So whose cases do we reject? Why don't we just defend everyone and anyone?

Believe it or not, most criminal defense lawyers are people too. We generally are capable of being subject to the same emotional reactions to various events and circumstances that real people experience. If a client is charged with brutally raping a young child, the mere thought of the act is so upsetting to me that I just don't want to deal with it. I don't want to cross-examine the child and beat up on him/her if she stumbles on the stand. Clearly, the accused deserves a good defense, but he would not be getting it from me if I were being too emotionally moved by the allegations of the crime itself. It is my fallibility and (gulp) sensitivity, and not my client's possible culpability, that prompts me to pass on the case.

Oddly enough, I don't have any such problems dealing with murders or other violent crimes. I can't rationally explain this obvious inconsistency, but over the years I have come to know what I feel comfortable doing and what not. I have come to learn that many of us have set up our own little personal boundaries.

I asked around.

Ron Kuby, often hailed as one of the real true believers in the criminal defense business, represented Colin Ferguson, the maniac who murdered eleven people one day on the Long Island Railroad. He also vigorously defended Sheikh Omar Abdel-Rahman, convicted of masterminding the first World Trade Center bombing. If he could fight like hell for those two dirtbags, he obviously has no such restrictions about whom he takes on, right? WRONG! I asked Ron the question. Whom do you turn down? And he said he will not represent anyone who has committed a crime based on racial or ethnic motivations.

Jeralyn Merritt of Denver was one of the trial attorneys representing Oklahoma City bomber Timothy McVeigh. She fought hard to save his life during and after the trial. McVeigh, having never showed an iota of remorse, was found responsible for the deaths of all those unfortunate souls in the Federal Building in Oklahoma City, including twenty-eight small children in the daycare facility, which *he knew* was in operation when he blew up the building. Jeralyn worked closely with McVeigh and worked tirelessly for him. But . . . she won't represent someone who is accused of abusing the elderly.

We all have our lines in the sand. They don't necessarily make a lot of sense to the rest of the world, but they seem to work for us.

Bob Bello of Connecticut is one of the best criminal defense lawyers I know. He has represented many people for murder, robbery, rape, etc. He also is the first one to step up to the plate when a friend or coworker in the system needs help. Without asking for a fee, a thank-you, or any recognition at all, Bob has been there to take care of the court reporter, bailiff, clerk, or lawyer when they wound up as defendants. What cases will he not take? He will not represent parents who sexually molest their children. He will represent strangers who sexually molest children . . . but not parents.

Gerald Shargel is high up on the short list of New York City criminal lawyers who are the absolute "go-to" guys if you are in deep doo-doo. He won an acquittal for John Gotti, who had been accused of ordering the murder of a union labor official. He has represented mob guys and white-collar people as well as the street guys. His response to my question:

"I don't exclude any category of offense. Depends on the client and the factual basis for the charge. For example, I just represented a female school principal who was charged with rape of 13 year old boys. Would I have represented a 40 year old man who raped an eight year old girl? Probably not unless I was convinced of innocence (that holds true throughout). So, it's not the crime, it's the facts."

David Chesnoff of Las Vegas represented a defendant in the largest controlled-substance seizure in American history. He is nationally regarded as a brilliant trial lawyer who has taken on impossible cases and clients. As of this writing, he is representing Las Vegas headliner David Copperfield. His response:

"Since I began practicing I have not been retained to represent anyone that wants to cooperate with the government. In the vernacular, NO RATS. I have always believed that if you commit a crime you should face the music, not snitch on other people to mitigate your punishment. Hopefully, I will do my job well enough that an individual's refusal to rat will still translate to a complete trial or motion victory in the case; or at least a successful plea negotiation. So far, after 28 years, so good."

We all were knocked over by the incredible job Roy Black did when we watched him win an acquittal for William Kennedy Smith in 1991 as Court TV captured it all, gavel to gavel. Based in Miami, Roy also took care of Rush Limbaugh when they found those four trillion pills in his house. Whom will Roy not represent?

"Bombers. Because they kill indiscriminately."

Dick DeGuerin is legendary, even by Texas standards. Recently representing former House majority leader Tom DeLay in his money-laundering conspiracy case, Dick represented Texas cult leader David

Koresh during his standoff with the FBI and the ATF. Most recently he won an amazing "not guilty" verdict in the case of millionaire-nutcase Robert Durst, who was accused of dismembering the body of his seventy-one–year-old neighbor and throwing the body parts inn Galveston Bay.

Dick's response to my e-mail was very specific:

"I don't represent snitches or hot check writers. I'll be glad to expand on it, but that's the bottom line. I try to help everyone who has the good sense to ask for my help."

What the hell is a "hot check writer"? Apparently there is a big problem in Texas with people who bounce checks or write them on closed or phony accounts. I didn't realize how big a problem it was until a few weeks after I got Dick DeGuerin's response. I walked into the Amarillo, Texas County Courthouse where I was representing someone accused of statutory rape. The first thing I saw was an office with a large sign above it that read HOT CHECK OFFICE.

Yale Galanter of Florida is best known as O.J. Simpson's lawyer in his "road rage" trial as well as the sports memorabilia escapade in Las Vegas. I asked Yale what cases he would not take. Conventional wisdom might suggest that any lawyer who could represent O.J. has no restrictions! Not so. Yale will not represent pedophiles. His reply to me was, "We have not done that type of work in 20 years. Double murder no problem. Crimes against kids—no can do."

Ben Brafman of New York City successfully represented Sean "P. Diddy" Combs in his bribery and weapons case. I watched him do his best to defend Michael Jackson, until Jackson's entourage and antics made it impossible to deal with the case effectively. He truly is at the top of the food chain in the criminal law business. I have been on several speaking panels with him, and I always feel like a total dunce after Ben explains or discusses the most technical legal issue in a manner that is both understandable and compelling to everyone in the room. I have often said that when he clears his throat, he is more articulate than I could ever hope to be. I don't know Ben that well. Yet, when I got slammed in a New York newspaper one morning a while back, there was a call from Ben at my office before 9:00 A.M., offering his wisdom and assistance if I needed it. When I was writing this chapter, I e-mailed him the question at 11:16 P.M. on a Sunday night. At 12:19 A.M., I received the following response:

> I have often thought about the question you pose. To me it would be a terrorist. As the son of Holocaust survivors, and with children and grandchildren living in Israel, I would be the wrong guy to represent a terrorist intent on mass murder, suicide bombing, etc. It is important that the reader understand that I believe a terrorist is entitled to a defense; it is just that I am the wrong guy for that kind of case because of who I am as a person, where I come from, and what is today very important in my life.
>
> I have no difficulty representing a real criminal, even a very bad person. There are degrees of evil, however, and I am not the right guy to represent someone who looks to kill because of twisted hate, as so many in my family have been murdered because of twisted hate.
>
> I think I am a very good criminal lawyer with real talent. My fear is that I would hold back and not permit myself to do what I do best in a case where the defendant is so despised by me. Hard to explain, perhaps, but it is part of who I am. I would fight for the right of that person to get excellent representation, but would never allow that lawyer to be me.
>
> If you wish to discuss further, give me a call at your convenience.

Like I said earlier, Ben Brafman may very well be the most articulate lawyer I know—and a class act, as well.

Sometimes it is not the alleged crime that turns me off about a case or a client. There are clients and cases that are simply cursed! In the *Li'l Abner* comic strip, there is a character named Joe Btfsplk who was always miserable. In every panel, he would be seen with a rain cloud over his head. Although he was a very nice person, everything just seemed to go consistently wrong for him. "Eddie Mush" had a similar fate. He was a very pathetic wiseguy character in the DeNiro/Palminteri movie *A Bronx Tale*. "If he didn't have bad luck, he wouldn't have any luck!" (At the track, they used to sell him his tickets already ripped up!)

I have found that if you do this job long enough, you develop a kind of X-ray vision that allows you to see the dark cloud that hangs over a prospective new client. It is there when he or she walks into the office. It is difficult to articulate precisely what the problem is, or is going to be. It is simply a gut feeling that this client and/or his case are going to be a problem. It may very well have absolutely nothing to do with what offense he is charged with, or whether or not he will be found guilty. It is simply a visceral reaction, combined with the information learned after hearing about him or his history. It likewise has nothing to do with the seriousness of his alleged crime. It's kind of like buying a used car with a history of electrical problems. It just ain't gonna work right! Who am I to reverse the karma? I am not that ambitious!

Another reason I may turn away a client relates to the very simple questions I ask myself after meeting him or her and making an effort to learn about the strength of the prosecution's case: Can I really do anything for this guy? Will my best efforts really make a difference in the outcome? Sometimes it is abundantly clear that the client is so screwed, it will not make a difference whether I represent him or he shows up in court with a real estate lawyer! I really like making money, but if I really *know* the end of this case will be a train wreck, I don't want to be there when it happens.

When deciding whether or not to represent someone, it is not a question of my pride, or a fear of losing. I just feel I am stealing the client's money if I give him any kind of unrealistic hope that the big check he is writing for me is going to really produce a happy (or less-miserable) ending. Oddly enough, when I explain this to the client, their reaction is often to want to write me a bigger check! (That becomes a real problem, especially if I really need the money that day.) The key to this issue is *honesty*.

So many lawyers go to the two opposite extremes in their zeal to get the client to write a check. Some minimize the case and foolishly assure the client that they can work some magic, and that everything is going to be just fine. These are the same jerks that tout their close relationships with the prosecutors and the judges. The other schmuck lawyers go in the opposite direction and totally inflate the seriousness of the client's predicament, far beyond the reality. They then tell them that their only chance of not serving twenty years for stealing that Kenny G CD is to write them that big check. Both lawyers wind up with the same result in the end: a very unhappy client who is justifiably pissed off and tells everyone he knows what a mistake it was to hire him. No check is big enough to fix that mess.

The new client interview can be an interesting exercise for both the lawyer and the client. I am trying to figure out what makes this guy tick, if he is guilty or not, and whether I can work with him. He is trying to determine if I am full of crap or if I am the lawyer who can rescue him from his nightmare. New clients sometimes ask me what I can guarantee them if they hire me. My answer is always the same. "I promise to show up and do my best." I also tell them that any lawyer who promises anything else is bullshitting them. I always ask if there is anything else I should know about them that I have not yet asked. I took that question from reporters who have interviewed me over the years about various cases. So often, this open-ended general question brings out a nugget of information that can be incredibly helpful in court or before a jury.

"Well, I did spend a year working with Mother Teresa in India."

"My father won the Congressional Medal of Honor."

"I am about to be indicted in another state for distribution of child pornography."

In the last few years, my increased visibility on television has generated different problems and issues for me when I am meeting prospective clients. I have learned that there are a couple of questions that clients are often reluctant to ask, but are clearly issues they want to have resolved before they decide to hire me.

Will everyone think I am guilty if I am hiring you?

How do I respond to that? Well, I guess I see it as a compliment. I must be so effective that I can get the guilty people off! I try to explain that if they needed heart surgery, would anyone criticize them for getting the best doctor they could afford? That analogy usually puts the issue to rest.

You are so high-profile. Will this case be in the news, or will the trial be televised if you are the lawyer?

That question does make some sense, but I still have to assure them that if the case is not newsworthy, it will not be on Fox News simply because I am the lawyer. I try to explain that the media follows the "big" case or the "big" client and *not* the lawyer, regardless of his television visibility.

Do you have time to do this? I see you on TV every night!

I do my best to assure them that I am still a real lawyer and that I generally do the TV stuff early in the morning or in the evenings. (This is sometimes a tough sell when I am wearing pancake makeup.)

Will you handle my case personally?

This is a very basic and appropriate question. The answer is yes. I will be the lawyer; I will not be assigning it to someone else.

You're such a big shot . . . Will the prosecutors want to really nail me just to take a shot at you?

Again, this is a very fair question. I do my best to assure them that I do not walk around the courthouse like some prima donna, inviting the prosecutors to take a shot at me. I explain how I "grew up" at that courthouse. I was a local public defender and a prosecutor there for five years. I came from the very working-class section of town, and I don't swagger around the courthouse like some schmuck. Over the years I have learned that most prospective clients often hire me because they feel safe and comfortable with me. If they have a positive visceral feeling about me, not much else matters.

Years ago I used to keep a Windsurfer at a friend's house, located a few miles from my office on Long Island Sound. During lunch, I would race over there, change into a bathing suit, and windsurf for an hour. It was a great head-clearing exercise. One chilly day in mid-November, I was windsurfing in a full wetsuit. When I got back to my car, I found that I'd misplaced my keys. I got a ride back to the office from someone and walked in with wet hair, still in my wetsuit. I had forgotten that I had some prospective clients waiting for me. They looked at me like I was from another planet. I made some lame explanation and sat down to talk about their case. After about a half hour, they didn't seem to care that they were talking to Aquaman and wrote the retainer check.

There are some clients that I won't represent because I really, really, really don't like them! This is very rare, and likewise, will generally have nothing to do with the seriousness of the offense or the possible guilt of the client. You don't need to bond with clients or socialize with them or even like them to be their lawyer. But it is not healthy if you really dislike them a lot. There is no way you are going to give 100 percent when you are hoping that the guy gets hit by a bus as soon as possible.

Sometimes a client will come in with an enormous chip on his shoulder. He hates the cops, the prosecutor, the probation officer, and the judge, and his arrest is part and parcel of a grand conspiracy to screw him. These clients invariably get around to hating their lawyers as well. They will try to impress me with the number of previous lawyers who have victimized them and that they have brought grievances or lawsuits against. I don't need to be next on that list. Even if I get a good result, they will still be unhappy. This is typically the plight of divorce lawyers. No matter how well the case goes, the case never seems to end, the client is never happy, and it's always the lawyer's fault.

Sometimes, it's the way the prospective client talks to his wife or parent in front of me that convinces me I don't want to represent him. Often, this is a young man who comes into my office with his parents. It's immediately clear that they have suffered through years of anguish trying to keep this kid out of trouble. As the young man is explaining why the cops have it in for him, his mom interrupts by trying to explain something relevant to the situation. "Shut up, Mom . . . lemme tell him . . ." I can't get this kid out of the office quickly enough. This never bothered me too much earlier in my career, but my Crappy Kid Tolerance has diminished with age.

I will never forget one client pulling the "Shut up, Mom" line while we were in front of Judge Robert Callahan. Judge Callahan was considered by everyone in the legal community to be the best in the state, and later, he became the chief justice of our State Supreme Court. He modeled patience and tolerance for everyone on the bench, and beyond. He had an incredibly unique ability to deal with every defendant in an appropriate manner—severely, if warranted—without stripping the accused of any dignity. He once told me about a morning when he was advising some defendant of his rights. All of the sudden, smoke started billowing from the defendant's pocket. He had lit himself on fire as an act of defiance and stupidity. As the courtroom bailiffs got the situation under control, Judge Callahan related that it took every inch of self-control on his part not to say, "and you have a right to remain burning . . ."

Judge Callahan was one of those judges who never forgot that he was once a lawyer. When you stood before him and your client was pleading guilty, he would always begin the sentencing process with: "Counselor, I just want to mention that you have done an excellent job for your client." He didn't have to say that. He just did it to give the lawyers a pat on the back (even when undeserved), and to let the clients know they didn't pick a schmuck for a lawyer. Judge Callahan also had an exceptionally sharp sense of humor. When he sat as a trial judge years ago, he would use the same hilarious line with every boyfriend/girlfriend defendant who would be brought before him for engaging in domestic violence. "If you two really want to fight, why don't you just get married!" This was years ago. The line was always funny, and served to defuse much of the anger and tension that the parties brought with them into the courtroom. Sadly, he would probably be chastised by some folks now as being too lighthearted about domestic violence.

His wit was not limited to roasting lawyers or defendants. There was another judge who used to sit in the same courthouse. He was locally famous for his lack of patience, and totally devoid of a sense of humor. Topping off these great qualities was his belief that every word from his mouth was the equivalent of the Sermon on the Mount. He was very taken with himself. One busy morning the not-so-funny judge walked into Judge Callahan's very crowded courtroom to ask him something. I was before the court at the time, presenting a case. "May I approach the bench?" this judge solemnly asked. He had a way of speaking that made it seem as if he were going to tell the sitting judge that the president had just been shot. Very important.

"Of course," replied Judge Callahan. The not-so-funny judge started to walk to the front of the courtroom. All of the sudden, he tripped on the court reporter's cable and fell headfirst against the bench. Everyone gasped as he started to get up, obviously shaken but certainly suffering a far greater injury to his ego. Judge Callahan didn't miss a beat. He stared at him and calmly said, "I said you could *approach* the bench, not *destroy* it!" That was probably the closest I ever came to wetting my pants in a courtroom.

The morning that I appeared with my crappy kid in front of Judge Callahan, I didn't expect any surprises. Judge Callahan had asked the young man some innocuous question, when his mom politely chimed in to clarify some point. My client turned to his mother and very impolitely and stupidly said, "Shut up—let me answer!" Boy, did he pick the wrong judge to do this in front of! The words were barely out of his mouth when Judge Callahan just about lunged across the bench, as if he were about to strangle my client. "Look!" he hollered, "maybe you don't treat your mother with respect at home, but you will NOT show her any disrespect while you are in my courtroom!"

I had appeared before Judge Callahan almost every day for about four years when I was a young prosecutor. I had never seen or heard him angrier. Judge Callahan was not exactly a slight person. A local high school football star, he had been drafted by the Pittsburgh Steelers, and later, he was a police officer and then a prosecutor before becoming a judge. He was not only articulate, but he also presented an imposing figure in the courtroom. Even I was scared! After the color drained from the young man's face, he didn't open his mouth again until he got into the parking lot.

Another reason I may not want to take someone's case is because I may have some personal connection to the victim. I have had several cases where the victim of the crime was a former client. On two occasions, I have represented people who have been charged with *murdering* people that I formerly represented. There really is no conflict of interest there, since I am obviously not currently representing the victim. I'm sure that sounds a bit cold, but it's the truth. Generally, the conflict in these situations has to do with the *comfort level* or *discomfort level* that might exist if I take on a case where I know the victim or their family, or have some connection there.

I remember driving to the police station one evening after getting a call from the family of a young woman who had struck and killed someone in her car. When I got there, I learned that the victim was a veteran police officer with whom I had been very friendly for years. There was no legal conflict, and the young woman was very much deserving of an aggressive defense, but I just did not want to face this police officer's family in the courthouse. Yet, I have had situations where the victim's family has urged me to take the case because they *do* know me and believe that I will not take cheap shots at them or unnecessarily vilify the victim in the course of my defense.

The social issues involved in the case may be something I do not want to deal with. A young man in town was once charged with painting swastikas on a street where many Jewish families lived. By all accounts, this was very much an aberration in the teenager's life. He was apparently a very nice young man who just did something incredibly stupid and insensitive one night. I knew some of the families on the street, having been active with them in the local Jewish Center. Would they understand that I was just doing my job? I doubt it. Did I need to prove that I was a genuine "true believer" defense lawyer who can represent anyone, regardless of the circumstances? No. I begged off, explaining my feelings to the young man's parents, and referred them to someone else. As contrary as it may be to the credo and mission of the criminal defense attorney, I just didn't need to be perceived as a champion of someone who had been accused of anti-Semitism.

Other social issues have never bothered me. I have represented both abortion doctors and pro-life advocates, as well as animal rights advocates and animal abusers. Playing both sides of those two lightning-rod issues is not a problem—with the exception of risking my life. The absolute fanaticism associated with abortion and animal rights often produces some genuine fireworks at the courthouse. While defending an abortion doctor who had been arrested after allegedly throwing dog crap at one of the pro-life demonstrators outside his home, I had to walk through a gauntlet of pro-life people outside the courthouse, marching around with those horrible posters of mutilated fetuses. Not a pleasant experience, but not enough aggravation to scare me away from the case.

One day when I was defending a man who had abused some animals, there was a large group of animal rights demonstrators outside the courthouse with the same kind of signs, showing tortured kittens and such. When nobody was looking, I posted a sign on the hot dog truck outside the courthouse: TODAY'S SPECIAL: VENISON BURGERS, SHOT BY LOCAL HUNTERS! I really did enjoy watching these people become horrified as they went to get their coffee. That was one of those "I really like my job" days.

Lastly, there may be very obvious reasons that I might not want to take a case. As the trial of Saddam Hussein got under way, a local Connecticut newspaper, *The News-Times* of Danbury, did a big piece titled LAWYERS SAY THEY'D DEFEND SADDAM. The reporter interviewed a collection of Connecticut criminal defense lawyers who all eloquently and very appropriately declared how it was their duty and obligation to take the case of anyone accused . . . yadda yadda. The article ended as follows: "Though most lawyers interviewed said they would defend Hussein, Stamford defense lawyer Mickey Sherman said he would not. 'Why? One of my goals in life is to not be murdered,' he said."

{Chapter 5}

The Jury:
Twelve Angry People
Who Couldn't Get Out of
Jury Duty

LIKE MOST CRIMINAL DEFENSE LAWYERS, I am a devout believer in the jury system—until they find a client guilty where I believe I should have prevailed. At that time, I bitch and moan to everyone about how crappy our system is, and what morons these people are who screwed my client and me. (I'd like to say that I'm joking, but it's the truth.) Generally, the system works very well, and we defense lawyers are great shills for American jurisprudence. Nevertheless, the system isn't perfect, and sometimes twelve apparently intelligent and rational people (six in some states) combine their intellectual talents to become a collective idiot. It doesn't happen that often, but when it does, it really sucks.

On balance, however, there is an almost magically solemn aura about our system. We take a group of strangers who know nothing about the case or the accused and ask them to decide who is telling the truth and what this person's fate ought to be. Once they get into that jury room, they take on their task with an amazing sense of responsibility and purpose. No film, play, book, or TV show has ever really nailed the incredible dynamic of the jury as well as the 1957 film of the Reginald Rose story, *Twelve Angry Men*. Superbly directed by Sidney Lumet

(*Network*, *Dog Day Afternoon*, *The Verdict*, *Prince of the City*), the entire film, except for one brief scene, takes place in a depressing, overheated jury deliberation room in a black-and-white New York City courthouse, where a jury of twelve very diverse men will decide whether a young Puerto Rican boy ought to be convicted for murdering his father.

What appears to be a slam-dunk case for the prosecution slowly unravels as a lone juror, played by Henry Fonda, ploddingly but deliberately shames the other eleven into taking a closer and more sober look at the evidence. Many of the jurors must strip themselves of their inherent bias against the boy because of their own personal issues, racial discrimination, or simple lack of appreciation for the fundamental presumption of innocence.

My favorite part, other than their verdict of "not guilty," is the last twenty seconds, which is the only part not filmed in the small jury room. Fonda is walking down the courthouse steps when, as an afterthought, he asks one of the other jurors his name. They shake hands and go back to their lives. This illustrates the genius of the jury system: Twelve absolute strangers come together to use their collective human experiences and common sense to mete out justice to another stranger. Most important, the film educates the viewer about what an absolutely awesome responsibility they must shoulder as jurors, and the fact that they better damn well be sure before they vote guilty!

I have never been held in contempt of court, but *Twelve Angry Men* was responsible for my closest call. How could this be? Connecticut is one of the very few jurisdictions where prospective jurors must go through a "voir dire" process. The unfortunate souls who couldn't get out of jury duty file into the courtroom, one by one. They sit in the witness box, and both prosecution and defense get to ask them pretty much anything they want in order to learn whether they want them on the jury. Based on the seriousness and number of charges, both sides are allowed a certain number of "peremptory" challenges; this is where we can just throw them out without any explanation whatsoever. Both sides may also ask the judge to excuse any juror from sitting "for cause." A judge will do this when the juror has indicated, directly or indirectly, that it would be clearly unfair to one side or the other to have them as a juror (i.e., their brother was injured by a drunk driver; they were once arrested and feel that the justice system sucks; they went to high school with one of the cops and would believe him, no matter what; and so on).

Before we get to question them individually, the jurors are brought out in groups of fifteen to thirty, and the judge gives them a brief speech about the case, the system, and what the trial timetable is. The lawyers then introduce themselves, announce who the witnesses are, and provide a list of their colleagues. The lawyers are not supposed to talk about their cases in any specific manner or *advocate* in any way during this process. But most lawyers will try and educate the juror a bit about the strengths and weaknesses of the respective sides, to see what the prospective jurors' reactions might be.

We know from the big cases in the news that anyone with a lot of money will probably hire a jury consultant who will sit in the courtroom, reading the body language of the prospective jurors. They may have conducted focus groups or polled the community to learn what the desired demographic might be for their side. They may be looking for left-handed Jewish art teachers between the ages of thirty-four and thirty-nine who may have a gay cousin in the New York metropolitan area. Okay, I'm exaggerating . . . but not a whole hell of a lot. Almost all lawyers develop their own manner of examining potential jurors. Too many just read the short bios provided and then spend twenty minutes kissing ass. "So, Mrs. Johnson, I see that you work in the loan department of County Trust. That must be interesting work?" *Uggghhh.*

I always ask what TV shows they watch and what books they read. If they are reading *Mein Kampf* or anything by Ann Coulter, that is not good for the defense. If they TiVo Nancy Grace's show every night, I'll happily use up one of my peremptory challenges. No offense to Nancy—she's a good friend, and I'm a fan of hers—it just sends the message that they are probably pro-prosecution. Why should I begin this race from a quarter mile behind the starting block? I like to ask them about certain movies. If they seem very movie-literate, I ask them if they have ever seen the Kurosawa film *Rashomon*. It is the story of a sexual assault seen through the eyes of all the various witnesses. Each person has a different recollection of what they saw. I ask them about this film to prepare them for what I will later argue may be classically unreliable eyewitness testimony. (A bit obscure, perhaps, but in lower Fairfield County, Connecticut, a surprisingly large number of people know the film and get the message.)

My standard movie question is always whether or not they have seen *Twelve Angry Men*. If they have, I then ask if they thought the Henry Fonda character was absurd. (A side benefit to this question: I have often spoken to jurors after a trial who tell me they went out and rented the film after being asked about it during the voir-dire process.) So how did this movie get me in trouble? Well, years ago, I was picking a jury in a rape trial. When the first prospective juror sat down in the box, I began with, "Have you ever seen the movie—" That's as far as I got. The judge angrily interrupted me with, "No, Mr. Sherman, I am *not* going to let you ask about movies again. You did that in our last trial, and I am not going to let you get away with it again!"

Ouch! I had just won a serious felony trial in front of this judge, where he thought my client was totally guilty. For some reason, he was going to do his best to rein me in this time around. Whatever. This juror didn't seem like anyone I wanted anyway. Moreover, this juror has now seen the judge crap on me. He probably thinks I am some unscrupulous wiseass. I was going to use up one of my challenges—but not just yet. "Your Honor, I really believe this question is totally appropriate . . ." and so on and so forth.

"No, it isn't, Mr. Sherman. If you want to take an appeal, that is your business." He was really pissed.

But so was I. We're talking about Henry Fonda! "All right, Judge— then may I just finish the question so it is preserved for the record?"

"Yes . . . but I am instructing this juror *not* to answer your question."

"Thank you. Mr. Schlepper, have you ever seen the movie . . . *Abbott and Costello Meet Frankenstein?*" The judge just about jumped over the bench to strangle me. The scary thing about this story is that I would do the same thing tomorrow.

Everyone seems to want to get out of jury duty. They whine incessantly about having to go down to the courthouse where they will have to mix with horrible people (me and my colleagues) who inhabit this scummy world that is asking them to fulfill their duty as a citizen in our free country. They bring notes from their urologist saying they have to go to the bathroom every ten minutes. They explain to the judge that if they miss four days of work, their families will starve and their jobs will be gone. They wind up sitting on the jury, kicking and screaming. But then, the magic starts. They drink the Kool-Aid. They get into it. They *get* it. Regardless of how serious the charges are, they feel that adrenaline rush and totally focus on the evidence. They are a combination of Mount Rushmore and the 101st Airborne. They represent all that is American, and find themselves on a mission from God to make sure that justice is served. They will fight like cats and dogs in the deliberation room, clinging to their opinions and refusing to compromise if they have not been convinced of something by either side. It is a wonderful transformation.

The only negative aspect of everyone going through this epiphany after serving on a jury is that they then have to TELL US ALL ABOUT IT! I really don't need to hear the details of other people's cases. I have enough problems attending to the details of my own!

As I mentioned earlier in a discussion of the "big case," sometimes the jurors *do* know a great deal about the high-profile case, and that is problematical when it comes to finding fair-minded people, as well as weeding out those "stealth jurors" who have other agendas not consistent with simply doing their civic duty.

In selecting jurors and trying cases these days, another issue causes problems for the lawyers on both sides that had not existed before. It is best explained by this Nielsen Media Research list, which appeared in *The New York Times* in December of 2005:

	Title	Network	Rating
1.	CSI	CBS	11.5
2.	NCIS	CBS	10.9
3.	CSI: NY	CBS	10.8
4.	Without a Trace	CBS	10.2
5.	Criminal Minds	CBS	9.9
6.	Cold Case	CBS	9.8
7.	CSI: Miami	CBS	9.4
8.	House	FOX	9.3
9.	Two and a Half Men	CBS	9.3
10.	NFL: Saints vs. Falcons	ABC	9.2

The first seven out of the ten highest-rated television programs were crime investigation shows! Every trial lawyer knows that these statistics are accurate, because every juror tells us that their favorite show is one of those first seven. So where is the problem? Today's jurors have a very sophisticated, yet not wholly real, expectation as to what evidence ought to be presented by either side. Thankfully, I believe the "*CSI* Effect" works to the disadvantage of the prosecution more than the defense. When Robert Blake was acquitted of killing his wife, the jurors came out to the front steps of the courthouse to be interviewed by the media. The jury foreman, Thomas Nicholson, announced the following: "We couldn't put the gun in his hand, circumstantial evidence. There was no GSR. There was no blood on the clothing. There was nothing; supposition more than evidence."

No GSR? Circumstantial evidence? These jurors have become THE EXPERTS. They have learned that every case needs to be solved with

My sixth grade class picture. I can be seen sitting in the front row, second in from the right, with my book upside down and a sly grin on my face.

During my senior year of college I told my mother I joined the skydiving team. Then, I sent this picture home, with me posing in front of a plane wreck. I told her we had trouble with one of the jumps.

Me pulling *The Joker's Wild* wheel and being paid in cash by Jack Barry. The game show took the money back at the commercials.

Willie Dobson on his
twenty-second birthday.

Roger Ligon, Treyvon
Jones, the Godfather,
and Noemy Ligon.

Cyndi Lauper, myself, and the Iron Sheik (in full wrestling garb) in the video we made for the Sheik's court case. The judge loved it and I later made him twenty copies.

Getting a "Thank You" choke from the Iron Sheik.

Up close and personal with the media.

My wife, Lis Wiehl, and I, before her appearance on Fox News to discuss the Scott Peterson trial.

"Crazy" Frank, holding up his infamous sign during the Scott Peterson trial.

My press pass for the Peterson trial. I think the sheriff's office got a little out of hand in making sure we all knew these passes were for the "Peterson Trial Only."

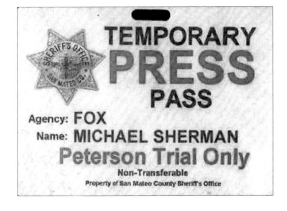

Covering the Peterson trial for Fox News with Lis from a rooftop studio.

Me, on Fox News' *Big Story*, copying Duane "Dog" Chapman's notorious sunglasses look.

Again amusing myself with my own sense of humor, this time on Court TV, where I donned a "scream" mask much to the surprise of the show's host, Catherine Crier.

The October 2002 cover of *Greenwich Magazine* (Photo by Fran Collin).

DNA and blood spatter and anything else that the writers at CBS come up with every week to educate and entertain us. Jurors love to solve the crimes themselves. They often come to the conclusion that the prosecutors and defense lawyers have missed the boat, and they can tell us what happened or didn't happen in spite of our combined incompetence. With the *CSI/Cold Case* expertise they have acquired from TV, they certainly have the tools to solve the case.

I always try and stay around after a verdict to ask the jury why they did what they did. Okay, I'm lying. If they came back with a guilty verdict, I leave immediately and sulk. Why should I give those assholes a second chance to make me feel like crap! When I win, however, I want to know what I did right, what I did wrong, and how these incredibly perceptive citizens reached their decision. As often as not, I am surprised as to what they felt was important and what was trivial. Clearly, the most enlightening information I often learn is how the jury basically disregarded my brilliant theory of the case, as well as the prosecution's version. They figured this out themselves, armed with their own deductive skills and investigative tools, which are often derived from any of the lawyer and crime shows on TV. Sometimes, their reasoning is right out of left field.

I represented a young man for allegedly raping a young woman he picked up in a bar. They had both been drinking and may have smoked some marijuana as well. Was the sex consensual? Who knows. He said yes—she said no. This is a very typical rape-trial scenario. Since the defense was consensual sex, DNA and other related forensic issues were unimportant. The jury either had to believe my client or the young lady. I didn't have a good feeling about the case, but I did my best. The jury found my client not guilty, and I was truly surprised. Relieved, but surprised. I hung around for the jury to come out of the courthouse.

"So what made the difference?" I asked out of the blue.

"Hey—if her family didn't believe her, why should we?" The other jurors nodded in agreement.

What the hell were they talking about? Nobody in her family had served as a witness. They didn't even come to the trial! It turns out that's exactly what the jurors were talking about, and apparently it was the focal point of their deliberation. When the victim testified, the jurors scanned the courtroom for people who would appear to be her family. They didn't see anyone who fit the bill, and thus concluded that she must be lying, since no family member came to vouch for her, or at the very least, provide moral support. This was not part of the trial or any aspect of the evidence provided from either side. Perhaps she was an orphan! How could the jury make such a leap in their reasoning here? The conclusion to this story is the fact that I shared this information with the prosecutor. After that, he made sure that his victims always showed up at trial with a parent or loved one in tow, or at least, someone who posed as one!

Occasionally jurors go a bit too far. First, they are not supposed to even discuss the case until all the evidence is in. So often I hear from jurors that they all discussed the case together from the very first day of the trial. The real problem is when the jury decides to do some independent research. I'm not talking about just asking their wife or brother-in-law what they think about the case on a daily basis. We saw what happened with Juror No. 7 in the Scott Peterson case. He was kicked off the jury when it became known that he had done independent Internet research about the case *during* the trial!

One of my favorite stories in this vein concerns the father of a lawyer friend of mine. He was on a homicide jury in New York City. I can never remember exactly what the accused was supposed to have done, but I do know what my friend's dad did. He drove down the street where this incident happened at a certain speed and threw a dummy out of the car to see how it landed. The guy deserves an "A" for effort and enthusiasm, but the evidence is really supposed to be developed *in* the courtroom.

As mentioned earlier, jury consultants are very common when big bucks are at stake, or when the accused (or prosecution) has the budget for them. There is some debate as to whether these experts can actually read body language like a book, but you cannot argue with success. Some of them have had great results in very difficult cases. Not that I need to blow my own horn too loudly (since you've already paid the twenty-five bucks for this book), but I was actually a pioneer in the jury consultant business!

Many years ago I had a client who was charged with raping his landlady on New Year's Eve. The evidence was a bit bizarre. The jury deliberated for three days and then announced they could not agree on a verdict. They were "hung," and a mistrial was declared. Six months later we tried the case again. A few minutes before the first witness took the stand, I stood up to let the judge and prosecutor know that the young lady sitting next to me and my client at the counsel table was Juror No. 4 from the last trial. I had run into her at a local restaurant where she had been waiting tables. She told me she had been one of the "not guilty" voters in the first trial. I asked her how much she made at the restaurant. Forty bucks a day. I offered her fifty bucks a day to sit with me during this retrial and tell me what she and the other first-trial jurors had thought of each bit of evidence, and how I might just be able to tweak something different to get the win this time.

The prosecutor objected on the grounds that it was, well, you know, because, I mean . . . There's gotta be some law against this! The judge agreed. They took a day or so to research the issue. When we got back in session, everyone had to agree that this was not "jury tampering" since this young lady was not serving on *this* trial and her jury service was over. Even though there was nothing on the books that said you couldn't give money to an ex-juror, in basic legal terms, the shit hit the fan. According to the State's chief judge, I had "undercut the entire system." Okay, that is kind of like a badge of honor for a defense lawyer. We're supposed to play the outlaw lawyer role every now and then. The president of the State Bar Association was very supportive of my innovative move. "The implications are so disturbing," he told *The New York Times*. Thank you, sir, may I have another.

Eventually, my actions led to the legislature of the State of Connecticut passing a law making it a misdemeanor for a juror to be paid as a consultant in a subsequent retrial of the same case, following a mistrial. It is known as the "Sherman Law." Hey . . . Jonas Salk has his vaccine, Mr. Geiger has his counter, and I have this stupid law. At least I am on the scoreboard.

Nineteen years later, in August of 2004, two California lawyers did the same thing in the retrial of two young Orange County men whose gang-rape trial ended in a hung jury. Like me, they were both praised and pilloried.

I still believe that juries generally see through all the crap and smoke and mirrors and do the right thing. There have been exceptions, but the world isn't perfect. The best compliment I get is when a former juror gets arrested for something and hires me.

{Chapter 6}

Victory
at
Any Cost?

THE APPROPRIATE ANSWER to this question always depends on who is asking it. If you are the accused or his family—we can never go too far to win! If you are the victim, one of their family members, or just about any talk-show host or guest—we always go too far! Johnnie Cochran was *out of control* when he pulled that "glove doesn't fit—you must acquit" scam. Of course, nobody wants to remember that it was the prosecutor who surprised everyone (especially himself) by offering the glove to O.J. to put on in front of the jury and most of the universe watching on television. All Cochran did was remind the jury how the *prosecutor's* stunt had backfired. Johnnie didn't create the scene; he just reported and exploited it.

Defending Kobe Bryant in a preliminary hearing, Pamela Mackey of Denver shocked everyone by asking a witness if the alleged rape victim's injuries to her private parts could have been the result of having three different sexual partners over the three evenings preceding the encounter with Bryant. *She is way over the line!* every pundit screamed. *She's gonna be sanctioned. The judge is gonna hold her in contempt! She's gonna get disbarred!*

For some reason, the judge took a five-day recess after that question. Observers and 96 percent of the 800 lawyers who shared their not-so-private thoughts with us on the cable news networks predicted the various ways Ms. Mackey would be roasted by the judge when the case resumed. How shocked was everyone when as court finally came back into session, she was allowed to ask that very question, and have it answered as well. Did she go too far? The world thought so, but the judge didn't.

Long after that trial I ran into Pam Mackey in New York. I asked her what happened when she was called into chambers after asking that question. The judge simply said, "I assume you have some proof of this?" She replied that she did. The judge then turned to the prosecution and registered his disbelief about the fact that they obviously knew about this too, and yet were still going forward with the case. Pam said that it was a very long five days before her conduct was totally vindicated by the judge. As my friend Willie Dow says about our profession, "If this job was easy, everybody would be doing it!"

So what are we *allowed* to do? What are we *supposed* to do? You really don't need a lifeline from Regis to answer this. *We are supposed to win*—without breaking any laws or ethical rules. That is the long and short answer. Sometimes we do use smoke and mirrors.

Here is a story that is guaranteed to piss off a lot of people, but since you have already bought this book, what have I got to lose? A client of mine met a woman at a local public tennis court. They wound up going back to her house and engaging in sex by her pool. She subsequently called the police and reported that she had been raped. He denied it and claimed it was consensual sex. Who knows what really happened? That is the problem with the "acquaintance rape" case. In the absence of actual physical injuries, it is very often a "he said, she said" situation that *must* go to trial. When William Kennedy Smith was tried for rape in Florida some years ago, everyone said he was only being tried because he was a Kennedy. Observers also questioned why the Kobe Bryant case could not be resolved without a trial.

Celebrity has little to do with whether or not these types of cases go to trial. These "consent" rape cases almost always go to trial—regardless of the identity or celebrity status of the accused. A woman has accused a man of rape. He claims that he did have sex with her, but that she agreed to it. There can be no middle ground here. If he claims to be innocent, he is not about to plead guilty and subject himself to ten to twenty years in jail. (It is very rare for anyone to get a suspended sentence for rape.) In recent years, most states have enacted various forms of "Megan's Law" statutes, whereby those convicted of sex offenses must register as sex offenders in their communities, on the Internet, and elsewhere. An admission of guilt not only puts them in jail for a long time, but it also stigmatizes them for life as the lowest of the low.

The victim of a "consent" rape case has stepped forward and made this accusation formally to the police. Her family, rape crisis counselors, the police, and the victims' advocates in the prosecutor's office have often supported her. She is not about to back away from her accusation. The only way this case is going away is by means of a trial. No prosecutor is about to tell an alleged victim, "Naaahhh . . . I don't think you're telling the truth. I'm dropping the charges." Even if the prosecutor has serious doubts about her allegations, he will take the easy way out and put the case on trial. *Let the jury decide* will be his mantra. He is not about to put himself into a very hot frying pan and get totally fried by every victims' activist group or rape crisis agency or the local newspaper. I really don't take issue with this process. I don't blame the prosecutor for not having the guts to throw the case out. He is not the judge or the jury. Who is *he* to decide the victim is not telling the truth? Frankly, these cases *should* go to trial. And they do. The only real exception to this rule was the tragedy of the Duke lacrosse players. In that case, the prosecutor *did* have more than sufficient cause to stop the bleeding and drop the case. He chose to ignore the incredible inconsistencies in the statement of the "victim" and played "hide the ball" with the forensic evidence that clearly vindicated the defendants. As I said, however, this is the exceptional case.

Back to my client at the tennis court: As mentioned, they left the tennis court and went back to her house, and ended up having sex by her pool. He left, and she went to the police to report that he had forced her to have sex. She had a very small abrasion on her body, which she claimed had occurred as they engaged in intercourse on the cement by the pool. He claimed it was totally consensual. We go to trial. It is a classic "he said, she said" case; anything can happen.

The day before the trial begins, I run into one of the detectives at the courthouse. We chat, and he asks me how I'm doing with the "MMGOOD case." I have no clue what he's talking about. He then explains that this is the name that has been given to my rape case by the guys in the detective bureau—because the victim's license plate says MMGOOD. Cut to a week later: The jury is selected. I have picked mostly women. When the defense is consensual sex, women are the best defense jurors. They will put themselves in the shoes of the alleged victim and often reason, "I have been in that situation, and I would never do what she did." Discussing the Kobe Bryant case and the believability of the victim in that case, Patrice, the very savvy makeup lady at CBS's *Early Show*, said it best: "Girl . . . you knew!" Like it or not, women seem to judge other women much more harshly in these situations. Men tend to feel protective of female victims. Absent any real physical injuries to the victim, and an accused with no prior history of this conduct, I would want the jury to consist of all women.

Back in our tennis court case, the victim has taken the stand. She did well in the direct examination by the prosecutor. My cross-examination is not terribly harsh at all. Contrary to what most people think, it is not common practice for defense lawyers to humiliate or badger a rape victim. It is generally a stupid approach that ends up alienating the jury and just about everyone else. We generally do our best to demonstrate that her recollection may be faulty, colored by other factors, or manufactured in some situations. Unless her testimony or conduct invites it, mean-spirited cross-examination is usually very counterproductive.

I finished my cross-examination by seemingly reviewing a boring checklist on a yellow pad. You left the park at what time? Was it dark? Whose car did you go home in? She told me she went back to her house in her car. I challenged her. "Isn't it a fact (that is the way they say it on TV) that you went back to your place in *my client's car*?"

"No."

She couldn't be shaken.

"Are you sure about that?"

"I took my own car!" She wasn't about to be bullied by me. The prosecutor began to enjoy my drifting into some moronic line of questioning that was obviously leading nowhere and making me look like a schmuck.

"What kind of car were you driving?"

"A Ford Mustang."

"What color?"

"Red."

"Who owns the car?"

"I do."

"What's the license plate?"

"MMGOOD."

"What?"

"MMGOOD."

I sat down.

A couple of days later, we presented our final arguments to the jury. The forensic and medical people had testified about the evidence. The victim's friends and family had testified as to her consistent accusations of my client. The prosecutor's closing argument neatly summarized all this information. He then asked them to convict my client of rape.

My closing argument began and ended very simply.

"MMGOOD."

The jury found my client not guilty of all charges. I hung around and spoke to them afterward (remember: I always want to find out what I did wrong or what I did right). Three of the women jurors told me that the license plate convinced them. Did I go too far? I won. That is what I get paid to do. The ending of this case is also classic. When I picked up the newspaper the next day to read about my great victory, my eyes fixed on the "black box" quote from my grateful client: "I can't believe I had to pay a lawyer . . . I was innocent." Instead of thinking of me as the latest incarnation of Atticus Finch, I was just another greedy, bloodsucking lawyer, profiting from the misery of the man on the street! The great New York criminal lawyer "Don't Worry" Murray Richman says it best: "We do the impossible for the ungrateful!"

An important lesson to be learned from this sleazy anecdote is where I got the information that helped me win the case. Most people assume that law enforcement people will do anything and everything to frustrate the mission of the defense attorney. I don't believe that is true. To be sure, there are some police officers who feel they are on a "mission from God," believing that we defense lawyers are vermin, put on this earth to promote evil. They show up in court on appearance dates when they have *not* been asked to be there by either side. They can't wait to tell the prosecutor and judge what a piece of crap my client is, whether it's true or not. This is quite effective, *unless* they do it pretty much every time they make an arrest. At that point, they lose their credibility with everyone in the system. From that point on, the information they put in their reports to the prosecutor is discounted by everyone, including the prosecutor and judge. Sadly for them, it's nearly impossible for them to regain their credibility. These police officers, usually very young ones, are absolutely in the minority.

At the risk of being accused of kissing up to the cops, my experience over these many years is that the average police officer just wants to do the right thing. They often speak up for some defendants when they feel they deserve credit for their good behavior and attitude, or if other facts and circumstances lead them to believe the defendant is entitled to a break.

A good criminal defense lawyer understands that we don't know everything, and it is no shame to take advice from pretty much everyone. You never know when you are going to get a nugget like "MMGOOD." Soon after I passed the bar exam, I was clerking in a civil court where two lawyers were trying a paternity case. The child was about two years old, and the woman was claiming that the defendant was the child's father. The father's lawyer was excellent, and it appeared that the woman didn't have a shot in hell of winning. She really had no proof. The man claimed that this could not be his child for a number of reasons. This was before the advent of DNA testing, and the blood typing available was of no help. The determination of the baby's blood type was not conclusive as to paternity.

I was bored and only half paying attention, but I noticed that the woman kept tugging on her lawyer's sleeve, trying to get his attention. Her lawyer was hitting one stone wall after another as he cross-examined the alleged father, with no success whatsoever. This man spoke very well on the witness stand and seemed to have all the right answers. With each hopeless question, the mother became more agitated and more determined to tell her lawyer something—to no avail. He kept shrugging her off. It was bad enough that he had this loser case—why prolong the misery by having to listen to this lady, who surely could not be of any real help at this point? Finally he leaned over and listened to her whisper something in his ear. Then, with the barest hint of a smile, the lawyer asked the arrogant witness four questions. Just four—but they were terrific.

Q: *Sir, do you have your wallet with you today?*
A: Yes.

Q: *Could you take it out for us, please?*
A: Yes.

Q: *Do you have any pictures in your wallet?*
A: (very long pause) Yes.

Q: *Could you show them to the jury, please?*

This guy carried pictures of the child in his wallet. Game over. (One could just imagine Howard Cosell calling this action: "THE DEFENDANT IS DOWN! THE DEFENDANT IS DOWN!")

I learned that day that you should *always* listen to the client. Maybe one in fourteen suggestions will be helpful, but that one good one could be the game winner.

What the lawyer should *not* do, however, is rely too heavily on the client's claims, relative to how strong the case is. A friend of mine was once representing a man for shooting someone after an argument. From the moment the lawyer got the case, he was repeatedly assured that the client had a witness who saw everything and would save the day. For some reason, the witness just never made it to the lawyer's office for an interview. Nonetheless, the client assured him he would be there for the trial to testify. When the trial finally was under way, the lawyer put this guy on the stand to vouch for his client's innocence. The classic question and answer went as follows:

Q: *And then what did you see?*
A: That's when I saw him not shoot him.

• • •

Sometimes, the only way to maintain one's sanity in this system is to take advantage of opportunities to get the job done and have some fun at the same time. Well, that's my theory at least. Years ago, the most-recent World Wrestling Federation champion was arrested on a minor charge in my area. Having recently lost the championship belt to Hulk Hogan, the Iron Sheik was driving down the Connecticut turnpike. He stopped to get some gas. Politely asking the attendant to fill up his tank, the Iron Sheik, who looks every bit a sheik, regardless of his attire, was met with incredible hostility by the young man at the pump. "I don't pump gas for Commie Iranian motherfuckers!" screamed the young man, obviously exercising his patriotism against the Sheik.

The Sheik pumped the gas himself and tossed the money to the young man, who claimed that the Sheik pushed him out of the way. The state police were called and picked up the Sheik a few miles down the road, arresting him for a very minor misdemeanor. They were incredibly apologetic to the Sheik, and clearly wrote in their reports that he was a complete gentleman. Although they believed *he* was the actual victim, they still had to make the arrest because the young man had made the accusation. This is not uncommon with a "one-on-one" complaint situation—the police will make the arrest and let the courts straighten it out.

After being hired to defend him, I learned that the Iron Sheik was indeed a true gentleman. An Iranian Olympic wrestling medalist, he had been a bodyguard for the Shah of Iran and was a hardworking, decent family man. The conventional manner of defending him would have been to show the prosecutor and judge what a good guy he was by bringing in assorted letters to the court, attesting to his good character. Surely the case would have been thrown out, or he would have been ordered to complete some type of first-offender program, which would have resulted in no conviction (and no other harsh result).

Soooooo . . . Why not do something different—and fun? We have all seen the interviews that these wrestlers do on TV. They come on one by one to discuss some upcoming match. They start out calm and deliberate, and soon build (or degenerate) into wild posturing and screaming into the camera about how they are going to pummel their opponent and what a creep he is. For some reason, it occurred to me that this is the way I should present the Sheik's case as well. The judge who would hear his case was known for being *very* severe, but I also knew he had the best sense of humor on the bench and would appreciate the effort. I ran it by the people for whom the Sheik worked, and they had no problem with it, trusting my judgment.

I showed up at the locker room of one of the big matches a few days later. They had set aside about twenty minutes for me to stand on a podium in front of a camera with my client, bringing on one character-witness wrestler after another. I told them the judge's name, and to just "do their thing." That was all the coaching they needed. They were brilliant. They spit, swore, and screamed into the camera, demanding justice for the Sheik . . . but in a respectful manner! The Sheik stood by my side in his full garb. He had been in a music video with Cyndi Lauper, who was kind enough to show up as well to help out. She stared into the camera and made an impassioned plea that came straight from the heart.

I brought the tape to court and the judge loved it. The prosecutor loved it too. The only one who was pissed off was the young "victim."

The case went away and everyone was happy. I made about twenty copies of the video for the judge, who, I was later told, showed it to everyone who came within two miles of his home. I have shown it to countless lawyers around the country at various seminars where I have lectured on innovative trial techniques. The reaction is generally the same: 70 percent love it; 20 percent are pissed off that I made a joke of it; and the remaining 10 percent think I should be committed to an institution. I continue to work on my numbers here.

Some years ago a young man from Texas was arrested for possessing a fairly large amount of marijuana. There wasn't a lot of wiggle room to deny the charge or challenge the search by the police. This was going to be a guilty plea and a serious effort to minimize the penalty, which may have been as much as fifteen years in prison. The young man was represented by Jack Zeldes, a veteran lawyer from Bridgeport, Connecticut. Jack requested a pretrial conference with the prosecutor and the judge to see if a plea could be worked out. This is standard procedure. We make our pitch to the judge in chambers in order to get either a commitment from the court as to what the sentence will be, or perhaps a range or "cap." A cap means that, should the client plead guilty to the charge, which the prosecutor has filed, the judge will give him *as much as* X months, years, or whatever. The prosecutor may recommend something in excess of that time to be served, but the judge will agree to undercut the prosecutor *up to* the cap.

Jack explained to the judge and prosecutor that this man was a college student with no prior record, and so forth and so on. He told them what wonderful people the parents were. The prosecutor, hearing such nice things about the parents, gave his classic response. He would nod his head in total sympathy and calmly say, "All right, you've convinced me—no jail time for the parents!" (I confess that, sick as that line is, I always laugh.) They finally finished the meeting with the judge telling Jack that he would cap the sentence at ten years. Not a big win. As Jack was leaving the judge's chambers, someone asked where this young man was from in Texas. "Alvin, Texas—wherever that is," Jack responded. The judge came to life! "Alvin, Texas? That's where Nolan Ryan is from!" The judge was an enormous sports aficionado.

Jack was a great lawyer but not a big sports fan. He had no clue who Nolan Ryan was. He went out into the lobby to give his clients the tough news about the cap of ten years. After a very difficult conference with the young man and his parents, Jack very matter-of-factly asked them if they knew someone named Nolan Ryan.

Cut to two months later in the same courtroom: They are there for the sentencing. The State lays out the undisputed facts of the substantial marijuana possession. Jack then does his song and dance relative to the good character of his client, absence of any prior record, work experience, education, and so on. He then begins to sit down. As an apparent afterthought, he then tells the judge that a family friend from Texas just flew in to address the court on behalf of the young man. Courtroom door swings open and Nolan Ryan walks up to the counsel table. He explains to the judge that he has known this young man all his life, and that if he and his wife were ever to die in a common tragedy, they would want the defendant to be the guardian of their children.

The client got a suspended sentence.

I never had the good fortune of having a client whose parents were best friends with a Nolan Ryan. I had to improvise. I happened to be in court one day when a colleague was making a pitch for a young man who had committed some kind of rich-kid offense. He had either knocked over some mailboxes in Greenwich or torn up a baseball field doing donuts in his Porsche. The lawyer handed a letter to the judge that I just *had* to have. It was a letter from former president Gerald Ford, indicating that he was a close friend of the family, and what a fine young man this boy was, yadda yadda. The clerk allowed me to make a copy of the letter. I whited out the name of the defendant and his parents. Three days later I had a sentencing with the same judge. My client was a Jamaican crack dealer with dreadlocks that stretched out to the courthouse parking lot. During the course of my argument, I approached the bench and handed the "President Ford letter" to the judge. I had typed in the name of my client and his parents in the most obvious and messy manner. The judge started to choke a bit and took a few minutes to regain his composure. He appreciated the gag and gave me a discount on the sentence for taking the time and effort to provide some entertainment.

Naturally, I beat the joke to death by giving the same judge the same letter at every sentencing or bond argument for about six months, each time with a new name typed in, as President Ford's close friend. It finally became so routine that he would ask me for the "Ford letter" as soon as I began any argument. On more than one occasion, other lawyers approached me to ask me what this "Ford letter" was. They thought it was some new legal pleading that I seemed to know about and they didn't.

Clients always like to hear that we "know the judge." Sadly, some lawyers prey upon such clients' beliefs that our familiarity or friendship with a judge will make their DWI disappear. It doesn't work that way. And it shouldn't. Other clients often like to see that their lawyer doesn't "take any shit from the judge or prosecutor." They want their advocate to be a real gladiator who takes no prisoners. Those are the clients who want me to tell them how many times I have been held in contempt. Surprisingly, I have *never* been held in contempt. Apart from the time I asked a prospective juror if he had ever seen *Abbott and Costello Meet Frankenstein*, the closest I ever came was when a judge (who really was an embarrassment to all of us) asked me during a trial if I was trying to show contempt for the court! I calmly replied that I was doing my best to conceal it. The prosecutor (who shared my opinion) started to choke back his laughter, but the judge didn't get it.

So how far will I go? As far as I have to go in order to get the job done. I will do my best not to cross the line, but sometimes the line is a bit blurry. I will do my best to stay within the confines of the law and ethical rules of conduct. But that is about it. Anything and everything else goes. Defense lawyers are hired to deliver a product—the salvation of our client. They have a problem and we are paid to fix it. I often say that I am much like a car repairman—hired to fix a specific problem, nothing more, nothing less.

{Chapter 7}

Hello,
I'm Satan:
Dealing with
Victims

ONE OF THE BAD PARTS about my job is the fact that I have to face the victims of my client's alleged crimes. Even if my client is truly innocent, it doesn't change the fact that this poor lady in court has lost her child because of somebody's violence. Like most defense lawyers, I used to just keep my distance from the victims and their families. I would avoid making eye contact with them and try to catch the next elevator if we were waiting in the hallway together. Eventually, I stopped doing that. It was silly. They know who I am and what I do; why dance around it? For many years now, I've made it my business to walk over and introduce myself to the victims' families in my cases, at the first court date. Their faces usually contort as they try to figure out what I'm trying to pull. I tell them who I am, and that I'm very sorry to be meeting them under these circumstances, but they should understand that I am just doing my job. I also encourage them to feel free to talk to me at any time if they have any questions about anything in this case.

Because of this practice, I have often found myself more in touch with some victims and their families than the prosecutor or his staff. I have had cases where the victims' families would call *me* rather than the prosecutor about certain details of the case. I'm not talking about serious issues here, but they would call to find out which date the case would be heard on, what time they should be there, that kind of thing. Not every victim is amenable to such civility, but I have found that simple kindness and open communication almost always make these situations a great deal less uncomfortable.

Sometimes, understandably, no amount of goodwill can bridge the gap with the family of someone who has been raped or murdered by my client. Years ago I represented a young man for the murder of one man and the attempted murder of a second man. My client had worked for these men, and it was our defense that one of the men had been verbally abusing and physically threatening him when my client pulled out a gun and shot them both. One man was shot in the head and survived. The second man was killed. The father of the young man who died was a local police detective. I had known him casually for several years, as I had been a prosecutor in town for four years. Our defense for the murder was extreme emotional disturbance, a kind of permutation of the insanity defense that allows a jury to reduce an apparent murder charge to the lesser charge of manslaughter.

There are two "victim stories" that came out of this case. During my final argument, I told the jury that the surviving victim was really responsible for the death of the younger man, since he's the one who started the conflict with my client. Although the surviving victim didn't deserve to be shot in the head, this tragedy could have been avoided if he had used better judgment. While making this closing argument to the jury, my eyes drifted to the courtroom audience. My wife at the time, Judy, was there to watch the closings and provide support. What was strange is that she was sitting next to the older guy, the one my client had shot in the head! They seemed to know each other and were chatting amiably after I'd finished my argument. This was beyond strange.

When the arguments were over, it was lunchtime. The jury was sent out for lunch and was set to begin deliberations after they came back in an hour. As I walked out of the well of the courtroom, Judy introduced me to a woman with whom she had attended high school locally. She was the wife of the surviving victim in this case—the one I'd just spent an hour trashing in front of the jury.

"Do you want to join us for lunch?" they asked. (I don't remember if it was the wife or the husband who asked, but we said yes.) It was incredibly understanding of both of them to be so tolerant of my role, and not to be personally offended by me. The significant part of this story comes next. Where would we go to eat? I suggested that we just hit the coffee shop across from the courthouse. Did it occur to me that the jury would be there? Naaahhh. For the next hour the four of us sat a few booths away from the jury, who kept looking over to see the defense lawyer having a pleasant meal with the man whose client had put a bullet in his head.

I think it was the next day when the jury came back with their verdicts. Regarding the young man who was killed, my client was found not guilty of murder, but guilty of the lesser charge of manslaughter. Regarding my lunch companion, my client had been charged with attempted murder. I had rolled the dice and successfully argued against the judge, giving the jury the option of considering a "lesser included" charge in the event they did not find him guilty of attempted murder. It had to be all or nothing with this one charge. It was nothing. The jury found my client not guilty, period. He received a sentence of thirteen years, served seven, and has been a model citizen for many years now.

After the trial, I wound up representing the surviving victim on some civil matters, and he has remained very friendly whenever I run into him or his wife. He still bears no grudge against me, and I don't think he has any issues with my client, who shot him. The police detective father of the young man who died never spoke to me again. However, he did show up and sit in the front row of every serious felony case I tried for about seven years, until he passed away. He would glare at me. It was unnerving, but I never returned the hostility in any manner. He had lost a son. In my view, he had a free pass to do whatever he wanted, short of violence. Oddly enough, the person he hated more than me was the surviving victim. He apparently agreed with my closing argument and blamed this man for his son's death, and blamed me for allowing the shooter to avoid conviction and a life sentence for murder.

There can be some disadvantage to developing an affinity with the victims in a case. First, as mentioned earlier, any sign of friendliness to the victims may be viewed by my client or his family as some sort of betrayal. While this is certainly not the case, I have come to understand the mechanics of this, and I try to be sensitive to it. There is some validity to the concern that if I have become friendly with someone, I may be less likely to be as aggressive with them on the witness stand. Likewise, even if I am not going to tear them apart on the stand, they will be less nervous about the prospect of being cross-examined by me since they have developed some level of comfort in my presence.

Knowing that my next statement is very politically incorrect and will surely piss off a lot of people, one of the problems in dealing with victims these days is working with victims' advocates. For too many years, there was a definite void in the criminal justice system where victims were concerned. The prosecutors would try to do the right thing, but too often there would be a lack of communication, and the victims and their families would be offended when they learned that some plea bargain had been made without consulting them. Over the last several years, the prosecutors have become very sensitive to the voices of the victims, but in my opinion, the machinery has gone a bit too far. The state legislators around the country, in an effort to remedy a problem that did exist, have created victims' advocates who too often fire up the family of the victim against not only the defendant and his lawyer, but the prosecutor as well!

When someone is accused of a crime, it is the responsibility of their defense lawyer to interview all relevant witnesses. This certainly includes the alleged victim. Every prosecutor knows that it is the defense attorney's right to at least ask the victim to speak to them. Most states prohibit the prosecutor from instructing the victim, or any other prospective witness, to not speak with the defense. Unfortunately, the victims' advocates do not understand or appreciate this issue. They immediately draw their wagons into a circle and make sure that the victims and their families see the defense as the absolute enemy, and the prosecutor as the possible blunderer.

My fundamental argument with victims' advocates has little to do with their disdain for me or my colleagues or clients. My real problem with them is that they interfere with the prosecution. The prosecutors dare not defy them, so they tend to deal with their cases accordingly. No prosecutor wants to be criticized by a victims' advocate! That's a public relations nightmare. Dealing with the victims and their families is certainly not the most attractive part of the defense lawyer's job. However, simple communication, common sense, and a bit of empathy go a long way toward making this part of the process significantly less unpleasant.

With the advent of victims' rights came the recognition that many court cases are "victim-driven." In other words, the prosecutors, judges, and juries are often guided not only by what the victims want, but also by how they present themselves, dead or alive. Most observers of the Robert Blake case believe that he totally benefited from the perception that the victim, Bonnie Lee Bakley, was not a nice person. Did she deserve to be murdered? Of course not. But were they as outraged as the jury in the Scott Peterson case? No way.

I once represented a young man for burglarizing a gun store and stealing all kinds of weapons. The plea bargain called for the judge to sentence him to as many as ten years. At the sentencing, the owner of the gun store showed up and went on and on in front of the judge about how my client had screwed up so many orders for automatic weapons and machine guns and God knows what. The judge inquired of the victim, "So basically, you are upset that you could not get these weapons into your customers' hands as soon as possible?" The victim affirmed this and continued to rant and rave. My client got a suspended sentence. Clearly, the judge did it simply to stick it to the gun shop owner. Hey—whatever works.

{Chapter 8}

How
Do You
Keep Your Sanity?

EVERYONE HANDLES THE STRESS and frustration of the criminal justice world in their own way. I know a lot of people who work out every morning, which somehow prepares them for dealing with the ups and downs of their life at the courthouse. I am not one of those people. First, I can't get up that early except to catch a plane. Moreover, I don't do well at the gym. While everyone on either side of me is on their fifth rep of jogging, pumping, or spinning on those machines in front of the TV sets, I spend ten minutes looking for a good TV station and then call it quits. Also, I seem to be the only one there without four bottles of Evian. And I refuse to jog because we all know it is the joggers who find all the dead bodies on the edge of the wooded sites, and who needs to have those memories!

So what do I do to cope with the stress at the courthouse? Simple—I add to it.

Some years ago, a couple of very nicely dressed men made an appointment to see me at my office about their recent arrests. My secretary hadn't asked them what they had been charged with. No big deal. I like surprises. They presented me with their "arrest papers," which revealed they had been arrested for "Wanton Waste of Waterfowl." Not being terribly worried about their concern over my inexperience with this type of offense, I calmly asked, "What the hell is that?" They explained that they own a decent size yacht in the affluent town of Greenwich, Connecticut, from which they often shoot ducks. They have proper licenses for this, and their guns were totally legal and registered. So where's the problem? Well, after they shoot the ducks, their dog jumps off the boat, swims to them, and brings them back to the boat. On this particular occasion, it seems that there were too many dead ducks for the poor dog to haul back, and a few were left floating in the water.

"So?" I asked. I still didn't know where the crime was here. It seems that you can shoot the ducks, you can have your dog snag them, but you *cannot* leave any floating in the water. That is a crime! It is a misdemeanor punishable by a big fine and a criminal record, so that's why they were there, asking if I would represent them. They seemed like very nice guys. They had a yacht . . . They're from Greenwich . . . This was not a difficult question. I think I had represented some friend of theirs who had been pleased with my services, so they were not overly worried that I had no idea that this crime even existed. Almost as an afterthought, they asked, "How much do you charge?" Very logical question, for which I had a very quick analysis and response.

"How many ducks are we talking about?" I calmly responded, as if it were a daily ritual.

"Sixteen," they answered.

"I normally charge $200 a duck." I waited for the laugh.

"Great—whom do we make the check out to?"

Those words represent *nirvana* to criminal defense lawyers. The only problem with a case of this nature is the fact that these arrests are not made by the local police. This type of crime is handled and monitored by a special division of the state police, who are responsible for offenses that deal with deer, lobsters, wildlife, and other environmental issues. They are very dedicated law enforcement officers, but I find that they sometimes take their jobs a bit too seriously. They not only make the arrests—they also track their cases like Inspector

Javert from *Les Misérables*. They show up at every court appearance to hound the prosecutor into showing no mercy for the poor guy who caught a couple of lobsters that were a millimeter too small. In short: They are a pain in the ass to the prosecutors, the defense counsel, and the judge as well.

We went to court a few times on the case, and finally the prosecutor agreed to dismiss the charges if the clients made a modest donation to a charity. The only problem was, who was going to tell the Lobster Cops that their case was being thrown out? The prosecutor agreed to tell them and stick to the deal if I didn't gloat too much in court. No problem. The prosecutor called my clients' case in the crowded courtroom. There were several lawyers sitting in the well of the courtroom, waiting for their cases to be called. A dozen or so prisoners waited in a dock, shackled together. As my well-dressed clients stood in front of the judge with me, the prosecutor began to recite the charges, explaining that he was going to throw the case out by reason of our deal. The green-uniformed Lobster Cops stood behind my clients, waiting for the ax to fall. It became obvious that they had not been told these charges were being thrown out. The prosecutor either forgot or chickened out. I didn't blame him.

The prosecutor recited the facts and circumstances of the case, and then explained why he was dropping the charges. The officers stood motionless behind my clients and me. Their grins turned to grimaces, and then to frustration and anger. In a vain attempt to appease them, the prosecutor assured the judge that he was convinced my clients had taken this matter very seriously and were very contrite. I likewise assured the judge that we all knew this crime of abuse of ducks was a serious matter, yadda yadda . . .

As we turned to leave and pass through the gauntlet of these cop wannabes, I opened my briefcase, tossed the files in, closed it, and walked past them out of the court. The judge started to choke with laughter, the prosecutor giggled uncontrollably, and the shackled prisoners laughed loudly. I had placed a large rubber chicken in my briefcase and closed it with the head sticking out of one side and the two webbed feet protruding from the other. Thankfully, the Lobster Cops had gone through the courthouse metal detector and were without weapons.

• • •

I believe that the finest art of courtroom chicanery is when you can get the judge to buy into the joke. I was once summoned to appear in court to begin jury selection on an assault case. I wasn't ready to start the trial, but really had no legitimate excuse to request a delay. The prosecutor knew I wasn't ready and was looking forward to watching me grovel before the judge. The judge was generally a very stern man who ran a strict courtroom and had no patience for ill-prepared lawyers. He asked the prosecutor if the State was ready to proceed. Replicating every kid we all hated in fourth grade who sat in the front row, arching forward, holding up one arm with the other to answer the teacher's question, the prosecutor gleefully assured the judge that they were 100 percent ready that very second. He then sat down and waited to watch me get beaten up.

I told the judge that I would be ready soon, but I was waiting for a report from a prominent neurologist I had retained to examine my client in his defense. The prosecutor jumped up—he had never been told I had any expert witness here.

"Who is the doctor?" asked the judge.

"Dr. Emil Shuffhausen," I calmly answered.

So here's the deal: Besides being a very strict judge, I also knew how good his sense of humor was, and that we shared several favorite movies. One of them was *Dirty Rotten Scoundrels*, wherein Steve Martin and Michael Caine play con men on the French Riviera. Caine's character's phony name in the movie is Dr. Emil Shuffhausen, *famed neurosurgeon from Lichtenstein.* I had nothing else to work with and figured I would take a shot.

"From Lichtenstein?" the judge shot back.

Success!

"The very same," I answered.

"Well . . . he *is* very renowned. You were lucky to get him. How much time do you need?"

"At least a month."

The clerk gave us a new date, a month later, and the prosecutor followed me out of the court, demanding to know more about this expert that everyone else seemed to be so familiar with. The judge and I waited about a week before letting him in on the joke.

• • •

Waiting for juries to finish deliberating is easily the worst part of our job. Well, maybe finding out our client's check bounced is worse. But any trial lawyer, on either side, will tell you how nauseous we all feel when the jury is deliberating. We are done. We have no control over anything anymore. We can't believe we picked these twelve glum-looking morons to decide our client's fate. We sit around the courthouse like the infantry on those landing boats in Normandy. In some jurisdictions, the lawyers are allowed go back to their offices and wait for a call from the clerk. I cannot bring myself to go far from the courtroom. I sit or stand there and stare at the jury deliberation room door. It is nauseating. What could they be talking about? Why are they making *me* suffer for so long?

Invariably, they knock on the door with either a question or a request to have some testimony read back. When that happens, we all become shrinks and immediately try to figure out exactly what they have already decided and what issues they are now trying to resolve. Even more absurdly, we all decide which of the jurors is on what side.

We give them names with appropriate points of view: "The Liberal Writer from Westport" is obviously voting not guilty. "The Jewish lady from Greenwich" is on our side. We do this every time, and every time, we are generally totally wrong!

When the jury finally does knock on the door telling us they have a verdict, a different set of old wives' tales (is this politically correct?) is in operation. If it is a quick verdict, it is good for the prosecution. Then again, if the crime is a serious one, it must be good for the defense, since no jury is going to condemn someone to a long prison term after discussing the case for such a short time. A long deliberation is good for the defense, since they are obviously arguing about something. These are all bullshit theories that we somehow subscribe to every time.

The most consistent Jury BT (Bullshit Theory) is believing that we're screwed if the jury will not make eye contact with the defendant or his lawyer as they enter the courtroom. About a month or so after I lost the murder trial of Michael Skakel, I had to try a drunk-driving case in the same courtroom in Norwalk, Connecticut. Just walking in there made me nauseous. My client was a very nice young man who unfortunately had two prior convictions for drunk driving, and there was a video of him giving the cop a hard time during the arrest. The jury would know about the prior arrests, and they certainly did not appreciate the officer being verbally abused by my client on the video. This was not going to end well.

It was a relatively short trial, and although the jury listened to my argument, I could tell they had already made up their minds. They knocked on the door and announced they had a verdict fairly quickly. As they filed into the courtroom, none of them could look my way. This sucked. I whispered to my client and his family that he would be handcuffed in just a few moments and given at least the one-year mandatory jail sentence, maybe more. They had all observed the jurors' behavior, too, and knew I was right. They began to sob as the clerk read that crap ever so slowly. After an eternity, they got to the "What is your verdict?" part.

Not guilty.

Is this a joke? Am I being punked? Where's Ashton Kutcher? How could this be? The jury foreperson could see my shock and was smiling. The other jurors seemed to have a smirk as well. Maybe I'd heard it wrong. When a defendant is found not guilty, the lawyer is supposed to ask that he be discharged and allowed to walk away. I was in such shock, I didn't say anything. Finally the judge piped up: "Mr. Sherman, do you have a motion?"

"Yes, Your Honor . . . Could we get some of those satellite trucks back here real quick?" (I couldn't help but hold that book upside down once more.)

I waited for an hour in the parking lot after the judge gave his thank-you spiel to the jury. I had to know what had convinced them that my client was not guilty. Soon, two of the jurors walked by to their cars, and I politely asked them, "How—why?" Their answer was simple and quite candid. "Your client was certainly drunk, but he didn't hurt anybody—and we thought you could use a win!"

Waiting for the jury to come back brings out the class clown in me at times. I once had a jury deliberating for several hours after we had concluded evidence in a serious felony trial. As jurors often do, they knocked on the door and handed the sheriff a note with a question on it. The clerk went to notify the judge and prosecutor that the jury had a question. When she left the courtroom, I replaced the note with one that I quickly scrawled, putting the real note in the clerk's desk drawer. The prosecutor and I moved to the judge's chamber, and my (fake) note was brought in. The judge told us that he had a note from the jury and it said (pausing for the drama, making us even more anxious): *Is the prosecutor a lawyer?* The judge immediately knew I had been up to no good, but totally appreciated the joke, and worked his way into the bit.

The prosecutor didn't know what to say. Was this for real? The judge kept up the gag by asking us how the jury should be informed of the prosecutor's status. Maybe we should send in the prosecutor's law school degree as an exhibit? Finally, the judge asked me where the real note was, and the clerk was sent to get it. Actually, I don't remember what the real note said. It was probably a request for a read-back of someone's testimony, which is very common. The joke was much more significant than any question the jury may have had.

Some years ago, a man named Richard Crafts was put on trial in Connecticut for allegedly killing his wife, Helle, by putting her into a wood chipper. With the help of our local CSI superstar, Dr. Henry Lee, Crafts was convicted after two trials. The case did not get that much national attention even though it met the first criteria of becoming a "big case"—it had a cool name: "The Wood Chipper Case." I had nothing to do with this case other than being in that courthouse the day after the verdict came in. Lynn Touhy of the *Hartford Courant* reported as follows:

> Stamford Superior Court Judge Martin L. Nigro presided over Richard Crafts's second murder trial, after the commercial pilot's first prosecution on charges he killed his wife, Helle, and shredded her body in a wood chipper ended in a mistrial. The defense had argued, among other things, there was insufficient evidence to prove Helle Crafts was dead.
>
> The day after the guilty verdict was returned against Crafts, Sherman, who had nothing to do with the case, noticed a flower arrangement being delivered to Nigro. It was from his wife, on the occasion of their anniversary. Before the judge saw the arrangement, Sherman swiped the card and replaced it with another that read, "Thanks for all your help. Helle."

A note about Dr. Henry Lee: Henry could get on the witness stand and give the traffic report for downtown Omaha and the jury would be as mesmerized as if he had just debunked the Warren Commission Report. He has incredible shtick. I know that is not an erudite legal term, but it is the only way to accurately describe Henry's immense appeal to the CSI-hungry jury and public. He is also quite funny. I have seen him work the same line in every case for the last twenty years, and it never ceases to break up the courtroom, myself included. It goes like this:

Q: *Dr. Lee, you examined the blanket (knife, whatever)?*
A: Yes.

Q: *And was the item given to you by the detectives in the ordinary course of your investigation?*
A: Yes.

Q: *And who was the detective that delivered the evidence to your lab?*
A: I don't know his name—you people all look alike to me!

He could be opening for Seinfeld at the Mirage in Vegas based on the laughs this line gets every time! An average day in a courthouse is really not unlike any episode of M*A*S*H: dark humor reigns.

My client is about to be sentenced, and the prosecutor asks me if the crying baby my client's wife is holding is their only child. "Actually, no. The kid is a rental just for the sentencing. Could you call this case soon so I don't have to pay overtime charges?"

I once was representing a man in his mid-sixties for drunk driving, his third offense. The law dictated that he had to serve at least one year in jail. He looked like crap, and I just didn't want to tell him there wasn't anything I could do to keep him out of jail. I came up with a genius plan to make the case go away without my having to tell him he was going to jail for a year. The prosecutor was Steve Weiss. He and I had grown up in the same "poor Greenwich neighborhood." He knew me well and was accustomed to my proposing some bizarre plea bargains. I knew *he* knew I was out of options here, but he patiently listened to my proposal.

"Let's continue the case for six months and see if he dies," I said.

"Is he sick?" Steve asked.

"No, I don't think so . . . but check him out: He looks like shit!"

Steve looked over my shoulder to the back of the courtroom where he saw my client, who indeed looked to be in terrible health.

"Yeah, you're right; he looks horrible. But what if he doesn't die in six months?" (It was a reasonable question.)

"We'll give him another 90 days."

"Sounds reasonable; let the clerk know the date."

Always appropriately concerned that he might be allowing a potential drunk driver to remain on the highway, Steve knew that if I claimed the case for the jury list, the case would be continued for about a year. By agreeing to a maximum delay of nine months, he was being as vigilant as one can get in this situation.

My client survived the first six months but died two months into the second continuance. I take great pride in the way I resolved that case. Not exactly what you see each week on *Law & Order*, but it worked for us pretty well.

• • •

We defense lawyers make the worst judges! This is one of those dirty little secrets that only people "in the system" are aware of. For some reason, if you take the most committed, compassionate defense lawyer or career public defender and give them a judge's robe, you often get an intolerant and severe judge who cuts nobody any slack and gives the worst sentences. I don't think I am alone in this observation. To make things even more absurd, it turns out the best judges are ex-prosecutors! To be even more specific, the best ex-prosecutor state judges are often ex-federal prosecutors who have little or no experience in the state courts, dealing with essentially street crime. These judges bring a practiced and often very patient manner to the bench that comes from the professionalism that they have been accustomed to in the federal courts.

So why do people like me suck when we get on the bench? We are just as smart as the prosecutors, and have certainly seen more clearly how people get screwed when the judges or juries make the wrong call. I think we defense lawyers have just heard too much bullshit from too many people for too many years. By the time we become judges, we have learned that we can't believe anyone. Our cynicism seems to overshadow our years of commitment to making the system bend a bit toward the accused. When we become judges, we are often too impatient with other lawyers. We seem to think that they all should be as brilliant as we were when they try their cases. No matter how good they are, they are not as good as we were. It is kind of like the George Carlin routine about what we think when we drive on the highway. "Everyone going slower than us is a *moron* and everyone going faster than us is a *maniac!*" We are the only ones who can do it right!

I have always said that what bothers me most about being a criminal lawyer is *how little it actually does bother me!* I think we become very much like oncologists—desensitized to the horror and sadness we deal with on a daily basis. I will listen to a client describe the most painful and heartbreaking story and rarely find myself moved. Instead, I sit there breaking his story down in terms of how it will play before a jury, or what defense is available. I often think that a normal person would be sobbing. I guess it may be a defense mechanism of sorts that allows us to focus on the problem and the solution without personalizing it. I'm sure it's a good thing to some extent, and a necessary tool in dealing with the job, but I always question whether or not it is worth giving up some measure of humanity in order to be an effective defense lawyer.

Unfortunately, we can't always hide under the covers. Many years ago I was picking a jury for a murder trial that was getting some press every day. My client was a young man from an affluent community who was accused of picking up a prostitute and killing her for no apparent reason. Very scary. Weeks earlier I had agreed to speak at a junior high school about the world of criminal lawyers. Since the jury selection process is often as exciting as watching paint dry, I was happy to run over to the school to give the speech during the court lunch recess.

I gave a little speech about the role of the defense lawyer and then asked for questions. The first one was the standard *How can you defend people when you know* . . . The second question was from a young girl who asked me if I was the lawyer representing the young man on trial for murder that she'd read about in the paper that morning. I said I was. She then asked me what the case was about. I basically repeated what was in that day's headline. "He is charged with murdering a prostitute." She remained standing, quivered just a bit, and tears welled up in her eyes. "She was not a prostitute! How can you say that? She was my mother!" I can't remember ever feeling smaller in my life. The teachers ushered all the kids out and I spent a long time with the girl, explaining and apologizing and trying not to cry. I got back to court a half hour late. The judge was waiting on the bench and asked me why he should not hold me in contempt and fine me or put me in jail for making everyone wait. I told him, in open court, that he would be doing me a favor by locking me up at that point. I explained what had happened. I went home and tried to figure out if it was too late to become a snowboarding instructor. What went wrong that day (or, maybe, what went right) was that I got a wake-up call, letting me know that there are living, breathing people out there who are affected by the bad acts of the people I represent. They are not merely names in police reports; they exist, and their kids do too. I will always remember the sadness in that little girl's face. Fifteen years later, shortly before this book went to print, I ran into her again. I was getting into my car at a bookstore when this young woman pulled up beside me and said, "Excuse me, aren't you Mickey Sherman?"

"Yes," I replied, expecting to hear her tell me that she had a friend who got screwed in court and needed my help, or that she was a friend of a client, or that she watches me on TV. My ego knows no bounds. I waited for her to say something of that sort.

"You were the lawyer for that guy who murdered my mother."

It was that little girl! She was all grown up. I stumbled out of my car and walked over to her. I honestly don't remember what she said after that because she was totally unnerved and was doing her best to console *me*! I was staring at her with tears coming down my face. I was a mess. I was being given a second chance to tell her how sorry I was about calling her slain mother a prostitute in front of her seventh-grade class. She assured me that she had come to terms with the loss of her mother and the fact that her mother had serious issues. We talked for a long while and I hugged her when we said good-bye. It was a very bizarre encounter—kind of like a "Dr. Phil Moment" in the Twilight Zone.

Then again, I have easily had more good experiences than the horrendous one described above. Years ago I represented a local high school math teacher who was accused of fondling a girl in school, basically in front of the whole class. She was a young white girl whose father was a police officer. The father had come into the school and just about punched out the principal upon hearing about the incident. My client, with whom I had gone to high school, was a large black man. The prosecution of this case was certainly not driven by racial motives, but it was a difficult scenario to deal with under any circumstances. And with a jury, you never know how much of a role the race card will play.

I called every kid in the class to the stand to testify about what had happened. With twenty-four different witnesses, we had twenty-four different versions. The case was won when I brought in the attendance clerk of the school, who showed the jury that at least three of the kids who testified they had seen the crime had *skipped school that day*! The verdict took up the top of the front page of the local newspaper. Sex sells papers.

That night my family and I went to get some dinner at a local pizza place. As the young black busboy was clearing the pizza pans, he looked at me, paused and smiled, and slowly said, "You're Sherman! You saved a man's life today!" I have been paid large sums of money over the years to represent many people in trouble. That is certainly one of the benefits of being somewhat successful in this business. However, no check for any amount of money could ever compare to the reward of that young man's declaration!

{Chapter 9}

Do High-Profile Cases

Get Fair Trials?

NOT LONG AGO, I was having dinner with my soon-to-be stepdaughter, a bright seven-year-old named Dani, during a family ski vacation in Colorado. It was Presidents' Week, and the adults on the trip were doing their best to keep the kids from being too bored at the restaurant.

"So, Dani, this is Presidents' Week; can you name one of the presidents we are honoring?"

"Lincoln!" she shouted right back.

"Okay—and what was he famous for?"

"He freed the slaves!"

"Good. And how did he die?"

"He got shot!"

"Where?"

"In the head!"

"No—I mean, where *was* he when he got shot?"

Very slight pause. "In the theater!"

"Excellent. Okay—and who shot him?"

"SCOTT PETERSON!"

Such is the total pervasiveness of high-profile trials these days. Once hooked, we become incredibly addicted to these cases. Every criminal lawyer in the country cannot take three steps without being asked to explain how this or that case is going. Nothing is off limits.

Even though the Peterson case dealt with the tragic murder of two people, it was Jay Leno's best material every night on network television. For most people in this country, the criminal justice system never existed before O.J. It's like nobody ever went to trial before the media discovered that the public could be obsessed with the trial of a famous football player.

And did the TV people ever win the lottery with that case! They had hours . . . days . . . weeks . . . months of the best programming imaginable, along with incredible ratings. They paid *nothing* for it other than the cost of the cameras and crews. The stars of the show were the players in the trial, to whom they didn't pay a cent. Even better, they recruited lawyers from everywhere who basically lined up around the block at every studio to dissect every moment of the trial, demonstrating their (our) incredible insight into every blink of Johnnie Cochran's eyes. We legal experts drove a very hard bargain with all the networks. We showed up at any studio that called us, for free! They did give us free rides to the various studios in Lincoln Town Cars, and all the donuts and soda we could handle in the green rooms outside the studio. There, we would endlessly pontificate during trial recesses, becoming legal geniuses.

Actually, there were some significant high-profile trials on TV before the O.J. case. Steven Brill, the visionary creator of Court TV, brought us gavel-to-gavel coverage of the trials of William Kennedy Smith, the lovable Menendez brothers, Betty Broderick, and many others. They were popular, but were merely appetizers for what was to come. The famous slow-speed white Bronco chase clued in television producers that average viewers wanted to see what was going to happen to this guy. Why? O.J. Simpson was a great football player, but that was a long time ago. His movie career wasn't spectacular, and he was probably best known to non-football fans as the guy from the Hertz commercials. So why did anyone care if he had gotten himself in big trouble?

My father used to say, "Everyone likes to see somebody else slip on a banana peel." With O.J., we had a very famous guy slipping on an enormous banana peel. It was like the entire country was in a really big station wagon on the turnpike and we'd all slowed down to a crawl to rubberneck at a horrible accident in the opposite lane. Since then, it seems that we just want to keep on rubbernecking. That is the secret (and the illusion) of the high-profile case: They are defined not by how important the issues of the case are. In fact, these cases are rarely important at all in terms of any societal concern that will be raised at trial.

What burning legal issues were present in the shoplifting trial of Winona Ryder? I stopped into that trial in Beverly Hills one day to say hello to Mark Geragos. We TV lawyers often bond like that. (Okay, so nobody else will talk to us.) I was the only non-journalist in the courtroom. The jury was not there to decide whether evolution should be taught in the classroom. The only issue was whether they believed their eyes when they saw the video of Winona stealing all that over-priced stuff! Linda Deutsch, the very accomplished AP correspondent, said it best when I walked in. "Welcome to the shoplifting trial of the century!"

These cases are high-profile because they involve famous people who may have screwed up (O.J., Kobe Bryant, Martha Stewart, Tyco, Michael Jackson, Diana Ross, and so on). When no celebrity is involved, they are just really bad car wrecks that we can't pass by without staring (Scott Peterson, the Menendez brothers, Jeffrey Dahmer, Lorena Bobbitt). The latter category is reminiscent of the way the media can ignore or downplay an earthquake in a Third World country where thousands of people are buried alive in order to cover the scene in Texas or Alabama where a five-year-old is trapped in a well. Given the choice, the producers (and the public) will go for the "kid in the well" story every time.

There are infinitely more important and legally significant cases being tried in state and federal courthouses around the country every day. They are being tried very adeptly by lawyers nobody will ever appreciate, much less hear of. Public defenders will fight like hell in "the pits" for little pay, no recognition, and virtually no gratitude. Their dedication is often rewarded with their client telling them that they did as well as "a real lawyer" would have done. But we don't want to watch those trials, unless they fit what I refer to as the Sherman Criteria for High-Profile Trials: No celebrity, no kid in the well—no coverage. Kind of like "No schlock, no service."

So what is the problem with the high-profile trial? Simply put, once we (the public) and they (the TV producers) zero in on the case, we corrupt everyone in the process! Well, we try to. . . Like red army ants in Africa (or South America, or wherever they are), we roll onto the scene with the satellite trucks and need to know everything about Joe Schmo, the defendant, or Mary Schmo, the victim. Reporters and producers will stampede over one another to get an interview with the shop teacher who once taught the accused in class, fourteen years earlier.

Who can forget the parade of "friends" of Kobe Bryant's victim that appeared on every network except the Spanish weather station to reveal what a party animal their "friend" was. We met Scott Peterson's former girlfriends, and twenty-eight of the young men who slept at Michael Jackson's estate and were never touched by him. This is no big deal. While not terribly enlightening, it often makes good (yet sometimes painful) TV, watching someone devour his or her fifteen minutes of fame. I once spent a week watching Rita Cosby of Fox News struggle through a five-minute interview of a hotel worker. This man could not deliver any answers remotely like the responses Rita expected, based on the pre-interview her staff had conducted. Apparently, the hotel worker did manage to get his name right, but that was about it.

Where we run into problems is when the media tackles the real players in the trial. Early in the O.J. case, a minor yet real witness sold her story to a tabloid for five thousand dollars. The prosecutors immediately denounced her and kicked her off the witness list, as her testimony was now tainted. When any witness for either side takes the witness stand, they may be challenged or impeached by the other side if it's proven they have some sort of personal interest in the case. If they have sold their story, then they have a stake in the case, one way or the other. They have a motive to testify: to enhance their story to make money. They come off like schmucks.

Even if they do not sell their story, witnesses jeopardize the value of their testimony by giving interviews to the media before the trial. It's simple—the more times you tell a story, the more likely it is that you will tell it a little bit differently each time. Each variance of the story becomes a treasure trove for the lawyer who gets to cross-examine that person in front of a jury. It is now common practice for both the defense and prosecutors to bring in TV interviews of witnesses to impeach them at trial. What is a great sound bite for CNN on a Tuesday night becomes a nightmare for the prosecutor eight months later at trial.

Prosecutors in the Scott Peterson trial were formally given permission to use in evidence several network interviews Peterson gave before his arrest. While it gave Scott some serious prime-time exposure, it didn't exactly help make his case for innocence! In an effort to demonstrate his heartbreaking concern for his missing wife and unborn child, he spoke of them in the past tense. The prosecutors maintained that this showed a "consciousness of guilt." We also saw him crying uncontrollably to Diane Sawyer on ABC. His crocodile tears provided endless fodder for discussion.

Sometimes it is not immediately apparent how important such a TV appearance might be at the time of the actual interview. When the western world was searching high and low for the missing Laci Peterson, Scott Peterson sat down with a local TV reporter from Sacramento to tell his story and plead for the safe return of his wife and unborn child. The reporter, Gloria Gomez, was very focused on trying to get Scott to either confess, or at least to screw up his version of the timeline. During the interview, Scott's cell phone rang. Without looking at who was calling, he switched it off so the interview could proceed uninterrupted. Gloria only realized later, after looking at her tape, how significant that event was. His wife was missing, and everyone was looking for her. His cell phone rang, and he didn't even bother to look and see who might be calling, possibly with the news that Laci had been found! Common sense would dictate that a man in his position would be jumping at every call or knock on the door. Was this compelling evidence of guilt? The jury was shown the interview and was free to consider the implications. How much did it contribute to their guilty verdict?

Every witness who previews their testimony in a TV interview compromises their value to the case, yet it seems that many couldn't care less. Such is the intoxicating nature of the TV camera. The families of the trial participants likewise seem to allow themselves to be seduced by the media. It is not uncommon for the parents or spouses of a recently murdered or raped victim to interrupt their grieving process long enough to let ABC fly them thousands of miles, in coach, to pour their heart out to Diane Sawyer at 7:08 A.M. EST.

On the evening of the death penalty verdict in the Peterson case, I was at the MSNBC studio in Manhattan, doing commentary. I ran into a very nice young couple in the green room. They had been the maid of honor and best man in the Scott and Laci Peterson wedding years earlier. NBC had flown them in from California to allow them to share their grief with the audiences of *The Abrams Report*, *The Today Show*, and other NBC shows. I spoke to them and found them to be very nice and sincere people. But why fly 3,000 miles to express your sadness to the viewing audience? The seduction.

I was to appear the following morning on CBS's *The Early Show*, for whom I serve as a legal analyst. I mentioned to the producers that I had met this nice couple and they should book them for CBS as well the next morning. Having done *The Today Show*, I knew they would be put up at the Essex House Hotel. I wasn't stealing them from NBC, just scoring some points with my people at CBS by trying to help them share the wealth here. This is not uncommon, and when the big stories hit, the key players often make the rounds of all three network morning shows on the same morning. One gets them early for a "pre-tape," another live, and the third, live or taped. The network morning shows are run very much like a war room. They must be on top of every story their network is covering, and even more important, on top of every story that the other two networks are covering as well. It is very much like the *Spy vs. Spy* cartoon that appears in *MAD* magazine. The next morning, I looked for this couple in the CBS green room. They were not there. I spoke to the CBS producer whom I had tipped off. Apparently NBC had booked this couple at the hotel with phony names. That's showbiz!

When the family of the victim/participant/accused doesn't want to appear on TV, they often send out someone else to stand in front of the podium of microphones that has miraculously appeared in front of their house. We have invented a name for these folks: family spokespersons. I have always wondered how they came to learn their craft. What courses do you take in college to become a family spokesperson? I think family spokespeople should be licensed as such. They should have to take a test or something. Unfortunately, not every spokesperson is really representing the party whose banner they claim to be carrying. Michael Jackson had to make a public statement, noting that not every person who was enjoying the hospitality of the cable news channel green rooms was actually authorized to speak for him! What effect do these interviews have on the prospective jury pool? We never really know—and that's a problem.

Lawyers are not immune to these pressures as well. There are ethical considerations that dictate how far a lawyer may go in making statements about their cases outside the courtroom. That is often not the problem. What I find odd is when lawyers go on TV *during* their trials. It's one thing to debate or spin the issues before the trial. During the trial, one would expect that the lawyers have more pressing responsibilities than taking the time to sit in front of a camera with a little plastic thing in their ear, talking to someone like me. If I was their client, I would be both pissed off and concerned that my lawyer was appearing on TV rather than reviewing that day's testimony and preparing for the following day!

In fact, even locations relevant to high-profile cases have enjoyed the limelight. After the O.J. murders, business boomed at Mezzaluna, the restaurant where the victims had apparently met that night. A front-page piece in *The New York Times* in January of 2005 focused on the shifting spotlights in the celebrity trials. Discussing how some celebrity trials catch our attention while others do not, *The New York Times* observed: "In modern society, there is plenty of money to be made in the misfortune of others."

Actor Robert Blake was on trial for killing his wife at Vitello's, a relatively unknown restaurant in Los Angeles. *The New York Times* reported that although Blake has become relatively obscure,

> Vitello's has become one of the best-known Italian restaurants in Los Angeles. "Business is good because of the whole Blake thing," said one waiter, an aspiring actor. "Curiosity seekers. We never used to have three waiters working a Monday night."

The communities whose courthouses host the "big cases" have done their best to turn a burden into a bonus!

● ● ●

Generally, we "TV lawyers" do our best to keep up with the latest developments in any case that is being discussed on TV. The producers send us the latest AP wires, articles, transcripts, "anchor notes," and other such e-mails, faxes, and FedExes so that we will have some idea of what we are arguing about at 8:00 P.M. that night on the XYZ network. We defense people will be pitted against a "former prosecutor," who will essentially tell us why we are morons and fools who advocate slaps on the wrists for all ax murderers and serial killers.

In an effort to be a bit more informed, I went out to the Peterson trial on three occasions to see for myself what the landscape actually looked like, and also to provide commentary from there for various networks. Having been to the O.J. trial and personally having lived in the eye of the storm during other high-profile trials, I expected to see the outside of the courthouse surrounded by satellite trucks and tents, from which reporters would be broadcasting every five minutes to report the very latest "breaking news" (which is always exclusive to whoever is talking). I soon learned why there was only one tent in front of the courthouse, with a bank of microphones. Apparently, the powers-that-be of Redwood City had been ready for the media mob to descend, and had greeted them with open arms . . . and a complimentary Bic pen to sign some really fat checks! They had blocked off, with tape, 12-foot squares of space in front of the courthouse and offered all the networks these cubicles for the discounted sum of $55,000 each. (At those rates, the Redwood City police would have been driving BMWs in no time!) Let's not forget: We are talking about approximately fifty satellite trucks and five hundred credentialed reporters.

But the TV people weren't born yesterday. They essentially gave the city "the finger" and scrounged their own spots around the corner, in parking lots and on roofs. A few attorneys allowed the networks to broadcast from their office parking lots or roofs for a few bucks, and a deal whereby those lawyers would get to commentate on television. Space for Face Time! That's what anyone would call a win-win situation! So every morning, around each corner and up on the roofs, beginning at 4:00 A.M. (the morning shows hit New York at 7:00), you would see bleary-eyed sound, light, and camera people being directed by young producers, together with their "talent."

Perhaps no group has been more "media-cized" than the only characters in this process who are supposed to be totally free of any bias, pressure, or preconceived points of view: the jury. We place our complete trust in their promise to be fair and without opinion or position relative to the issues of the trials upon which juries they have been selected to serve. They have sworn to us during the selection process that they have no opinions about the case or the parties involved. But ten minutes after the verdict has been announced, too many of them are in front of the cameras at the courthouse or on the networks, sharing their views.

Are these high-profile-case jurors entitled to enjoy their fame? No law against it—at the moment. But their guaranteed celebrity presents two problems: First, it forces us to question whether or not they answered all the questions honestly during the voir-dire jury selection process. Did they really have no opinion as to the guilt of the accused, or would they have said pretty much anything to get on the jury and hang out with Matt Lauer down the road? It's sort of like the legal-system version of *American Idol*. Think about it: You get that annoying letter summoning you to jury duty. When you get to the courthouse, there are satellite trucks everywhere, and Dan Abrams, Catherine Crier, and their colleagues are all talking to the air in front of the building. You then realize you are there for *the big case*. For a few weeks of listening to lawyers and such, you will get that plane ride and limo to New York, and you'll be the lead-in to Britney Spears on *The Today Show*. All those people with the silly signs outside Studio A in Rockefeller Center will be watching your every move inside, as you casually chat with Meredith Vieira like you were old friends from high school!

The second problem with celebrity jurors is that their post-verdict interviews with the media sometimes screw up the verdict itself! They may very well talk about the deliberation process and let us know that they or someone else on the jury did not follow the law. It is common for lawyers or their investigators to speak to jurors after a losing case to determine whether there was any juror misconduct. Did they allow prejudice or undue influence from sources other than the evidence to control their deliberations? Did a juror conduct some kind of experiment or visit the scene of the crime in violation of his juror oath? Well, we might very well find out when they tell all to Geraldo at 10:00 P.M. EST.

This happened right after the Martha Stewart guilty verdict, when one juror rushed to the bank of cameras in front of the New York courthouse before Martha even knew what hit her. He made a comment to the effect that this was a victory for the little guy, yadda yadda. Well, last we checked, he was supposed to determine whether or not Martha Stewart committed a couple of federal crimes—not whether or not the little guys should beat the rich ladies. Martha's legal team cited this "juror misconduct" in their appeal. We have even given a name to these jurors who so eagerly want to do their civic duty—as long as there are satellite trucks nearby. We call them "stealth jurors." Check out this Associated Press story from April 2004:

PETERSON JUDGE EXCUSES STEALTH JUROR FOR
LYING TO GET ON PANEL

REDWOOD CITY, CALIF. (AP) A retired woman accused of lying to get on the jury for Scott Peterson's double-murder trial was excused Tuesday after a judge met with lawyers behind closed doors.

Judge Alfred A. Delucchi dismissed the unidentified Redwood City woman after a brief meeting in his chambers.

Defense lawyer Mark Geragos two weeks ago accused the retired secretary of bragging to her friends on a bus trip to Reno, Nev., that she had "passed the test" to get on Peterson's jury and that Peterson was "guilty as hell" and he would "get what's due to him."

Geragos said a fellow bus passenger called his office to report what he had heard. The woman denied the allegations.

Both the tipster and the potential juror were scheduled to return to court next month for a hearing on the matter, but the judge's decision Tuesday made that unnecessary.

In March of 2005, a San Diego court was about to begin jury selection in the trial of Alejandro Avila, who was accused of kidnapping and murdering a young girl named Samantha Runnion. The entire community had searched for her, and over four thousand attended her funeral. "John and Ken," local Orange County radio personalities, came under fire from the judge in this case after they encouraged all those who had received jury service notices to lie about their knowledge or opinions of the case in order to stack the jury with "stealth" jurors who would convict. On the air, they repeatedly encouraged citizens to basically perjure themselves and thus corrupt the process.

It is my experience that jurors generally take their jobs incredibly seriously and really do their damnedest to do the right thing. Unfortunately, the seductive and distracting influence of the media and the unmitigated and unchecked desire for great "backstories" can often bring out the dark side of people.

In June 2004, Juror No. 5 in the Scott Peterson trial was thrown off the jury after a courthouse video caught him joking with the brother of the victim. Earlier, he seemed to be giving some kind of thumbs-up sign to the defense on a regular basis. Finally, after lengthy questioning by the judge, he admitted to having discussed the media coverage of the trial with his girlfriend and others. That was the final straw. The judge booted him off the jury. He landed on the run—running to every microphone and camera within a 200-mile radius. For two days, there was no bigger story in this country. Our troops in Iraq, the economy, politics . . . all were number-two or -three stories behind the many appearances of Juror No. 5, an airport screener named Justin Falconer who told us that the prosecution's case was so weak and boring, it was "driving him nuts." His best line was something to the effect that we all know how crazy pregnant women can get. His punishment for being so politically incorrect? Prime spot the next morning on *The Today Show!*

In the end, Justin Falconer did not get a book deal or a reality show (at least, at the time of this writing). But he did stretch his fifteen minutes of fame considerably, appearing regularly on cable news networks as a commentator on the trial. On July 19, 2004, I appeared on *Catherine Crier Live* on Court TV to dissect the latest high-profile cases. I was happy to learn that I would be joined by Juror No. 5 in our discussion of the Scott Peterson case. I asked Justin Falconer if his views of the trial were his alone, or did other members of the jury share them. Welcoming the need to validate his well-publicized and controversial opinions about the case, he told me (and the viewing public) that others on the jury shared his views. "So you discussed the case in the jury room?" I asked. My TV cross-examination was bearing fruit. As we all know, jurors are instructed every day *not* to discuss the case with the other jurors until the conclusion of the trial. Justin hadn't seen this coming. He tried to backpedal as I kept trying to get him to talk about how much they had discussed the case. Justin was ultimately bailed out by Catherine Crier, who was being kind to him (and also didn't want her show to be the basis for a mistrial).

Justin became a regular commentator on all the cable news networks for the balance of the trial. He was also there to weigh in on the guilty verdict, as well as the jury's finding that Peterson should suffer the death penalty. When questioned about why Justin's views of Scott's guilt or innocence seemed to be very different from the ultimate finding of the jury, other jurors were very critical of Falconer, claiming that he must have been at a different trial. Perhaps the judge should have instructed the dismissed juror *not* to speak to the media. However, it is questionable whether or not a judge has such a power. The dismissed juror is no longer part of the case, and he does enjoy a right to free speech. Again, the issue is one of balance. The judge must weigh the importance of the juror's right to speak out against the possibility of prejudice in the trial.

Before (and after) he became known as the "O.J. Lawyer," Robert Shapiro of Los Angeles had handled countless criminal and civil matters involving not only celebrities and rich people, but also any number of serious cases. Shortly after the Peterson verdict, Shapiro wrote a very appropriate Op-Ed piece that appeared around the country. Concerned with the issue of jurors' motives, he advocated, "Laws are needed to keep money from undermining justice!"

> Everyone, including the Peterson jurors, had to be aware that the national landscape is dotted with former nobodies who have found fame and fortune in the glare of the media spotlight. Former prisoner of war Jessica Lynch, who signed a $1 million book deal, is a good recent example. Consider for a moment the opportunities that arise if you are the holdout juror in the Peterson case. Larry King can't wait to ask you, "What was it like to be the holdout?" Katie Couric will follow up early in the morning with, "How did you possibly bear that pressure?" Just as the most obnoxious and offensive contestant on The Apprentice got his or her fifteen minutes of fame, so would the lone juror. Dominick Dunne would arrive on the scene for an exclusive interview in Vanity Fair. Could a book deal be far behind? And how about becoming a motivational speaker on sticking up for your own opinions, and the power of the individual?

(In point of fact, Private Jessica Lynch's deal might have been even sweeter. According to the June 16, 2003, edition of *The New York Times*, the major networks executives' pitch to Lynch for her exclusive cooperation in the production of a two-hour documentary was truly unique. In addition to the book deal, she and her friends would also host a special one-hour MTV show. MTV would also feature her in a special edition of their show *Total Request Live*, broadcast live from her home in Palestine, West Virginia. Her guests would include Ashanti and Ja Rule.)

Shapiro's prophecy really came to life a year later, after the Michael Jackson trial. Michael Jackson was found not guilty on June 13, 2005.

Within weeks, two jurors were already shopping scripts. According to the August 29, 2005, edition of the *New York Post*, the respective scripts, *The Deliberator* and *Guilty as Sin, Free as a Bird*, share a common theme: These two jurors were bullied by the other jurors into finding Jackson not guilty! In response, five other Jackson jurors announced that they would also be pushing their own deliberation-room tell-all books. Angered by the first two enterprising jurors, one of the five, Michael Stevens, an aspiring sports journalist, was quoted as saying, "We just want to set the record straight." Right—and it wouldn't hurt to jump on the gravy train. Seven out of twelve jurors looking for book and movie deals! What is wrong with this picture?

Things got even worse with the Peterson jury. The trial had begun on June 1, 2004, after over three months of jury selection. Juror No. 5, the now almost-famous Justin Falconer, was dismissed from the case on June 23 (over the objections of the defense). The jury was finally given the case on November 4, when they were sequestered. We all waited. After five days of deliberation, the court convened to make an announcement. Instead of a verdict, the judge informed everyone that he was kicking another juror off the panel. Apparently, Juror No. 7 had conducted independent research on the Internet about the case and had obviously shared this knowledge with other jurors! There was more to come.

The next day, November 10, the wheels started flying off. Over another objection by the defense, the new Juror No. 5 (who had taken Justin Falconer's number when Falconer was kicked off) was also dismissed by the judge. Gregory Jackson, a lawyer and a doctor, had filled multiple notebooks with his observations. The conventional wisdom of all the pundits was that, given his pedigree, he was the ideal natural leader of the jury—and indeed, he had been serving as jury foreman. What could have prompted Jackson's removal? He apparently asked to be removed from the jury because of "an enormous amount of hostility" directed toward him. He told Judge Delucchi that comments made to him personally caused him to believe that his personal safety might be at risk, and because of the perceived hostility, he may be too prejudiced to continue his duty as a juror, let alone as foreman. What Gregory Jackson told the judge is essentially the storyboard for the hazards of the "media-cization" of the big case:

> When I took the oath, I understood it to mean that I needed to be able to weigh both sides fairly, openly. And given what's transpired, my individual ability to do that, I think, has been compromised to a degree that I would never know personally whether or not I was giving the community's verdict, the popular verdict, the expected verdict, the verdict that might, I don't know, produce the best book. I'm not going to speak to the media. I don't ever want to personally profit from this case in any way, directly or indirectly.

Within a few hours of Gregory Jackson's dismissal, the balance of the jury returned with a guilty verdict. Defense attorney Mark Geragos moved that the court dismiss this jury and convene a new one for the sentencing phase of the trial. Citing the above statement by Jackson, Geragos claimed that the dismissed juror—and logically, all the others—had been under improper pressure to render a verdict that "reflected the community's interest."

"In other words," Geragos argued in his motion, "pressures from the 'lynch mob' had invaded the jury box even before the mob had itself assembled outside the courthouse." Was it a lynch mob outside the courthouse? Should the judge have continued to sequester the jury so that they would not see the euphoria of the community—and the nation—at their verdict? Did they then feel the pressure to further satiate the mob by sentencing Peterson to death? We all saw those crowds outside, cheering at the announcement of the verdict. People honked their horns, high-fived each other, and basically replicated the old newsreels of the crowds in large cities reacting to the news of the end of World War II. Look at the front page of the *Redwood City News* that day: Was the headline any bigger for Pearl Harbor or September 11? I seriously doubt it.

Geragos faulted the judge for allowing the jurors to see the community reaction to their verdict of guilty. He claimed that they were "presumptively disabled" from impartially deciding Peterson's sentence. The appellate courts will ultimately make that call. It may very well be a close one. In the Peterson case, the judge took a baby step toward dealing with these issues. He forbade the jurors from accepting *any* compensation (including plane tickets and limos) from anyone for ninety days following the end of the case. It had been reported that the networks had chartered jets fueled and ready to speed jurors to the New York City morning-show newsrooms. Did ninety days make a big difference? The way I see it, he just gave them more time for the book agents to make their deals!

Juror No. 7 in the Peterson case became known as "Strawberry Shortcake" by reason of her colorful attire and . . . interesting hair. Perhaps proving Geragos's argument that these jurors were basically "on a mission from God," she wrote a lengthy article that appeared in the *New York Post* less than forty-eight hours after she voted to put Scott Peterson to death.

Was the verdict influenced by the anticipated public scrutiny of the jury's product? Should we place limits on how much they can profit from their jury service? Seven of the Peterson jurors eventually combined to produce the book *We, the Jury: Deciding the Scott Peterson Case*, which was published in January of 2007. It did pretty well.

• • •

The high-profile case does present a host of issues not found in the cases we don't hear (or seem to care) about. But this is not an argument against the televising of trials. The issue of cameras in the courtroom has been widely debated. In 1989, I got a call from someone working for Steven Brill, the publisher of *American Lawyer* and at least fifteen other state legal publications around the country. He was going to create a TV network where they just showed live trials from around the country. He asked if I would come down to the HBO studios in New York City and sit there and pontificate about some trial they would be showing as a pilot for the network.

I was introduced to Fred Graham, former host of CBS's *Face the Nation*. Another lawyer and I would sit on the set with him, watching a trial in Kentucky where some schoolchildren were incinerated when their bus was in a horrible accident. It seemed to go well. Everyone was running around terrified that Mr. Brill was going to holler at them, or at least give them a dirty look (which, if you know Steve Brill, can be even scarier). Fred Graham was very nice and very professional, compared to what I had been used to. I tried my best not to make any fart jokes or refer to things that I'd heard on Howard Stern's show that morning. The other lawyer was Barry Sheck. Barry was . . . well, he was Barry Sheck. When I was taking a break to call my office to find out how many new DWIs had come in that day, Barry was probably calling the governor of Alabama to confirm that he was saving another innocent man from the gas chamber. Okay, maybe I am exaggerating—but not a whole lot. At the end of the day, Barry and I left, agreeing that nobody was ever going to want to watch trials all day long.

WRONG! Court TV went on the air on July 1, 1990. I was there again with Fred doing commentary. And Steve Brill was there, glaring at everyone when things went wrong. But things went right. Very soon we saw Marlon Brando's son, Christian, being sentenced to ten years for killing the guy who was beating up his sister. Bob Shapiro was his lawyer. Like a Dickens novel, where all the characters come back later in the book, Brando came back in 2003 as a potential suspect in the murder of Bonnie Lee Bakley, the wife of Robert Blake. Shapiro, of course, came back for O.J.

A case of mine, *Connecticut v. Roger Ligon*, was one of the first full-length "taped trials" covered by Court TV (and somewhat exceptional in that I was using an insanity defense for my client—not known for its high success ratio). The trial was taped by Court TV and CBS before the network went on air on July 1, 1990, and aired shortly after that. I found the experience of trying a case on TV enormously fascinating, and did my best to use the TV process rather than be intimidated or spooked by it. The prosecutor and I both wore lapel microphones. If I wanted to say something to my client (or anyone else, for that matter) without sharing my thoughts with a room full of media people, I had to switch off the little gizmo on my belt.

One day during the trial, the prosecutor had done something he regretted; it was really nothing, and I honestly have no recollection as to what it was. Suffice it to say that the prosecutor felt he had screwed something up. We went into chambers with the judge. The prosecutor walked in saying, "I cannot believe what an asshole I am!" I looked at him and frantically pointed to his microphone switch, which he had neglected to turn off. His torment was compounded by the knowledge that his comment had been nicely recorded by CBS, Court TV, and *Dateline*. Now he *really* felt like an asshole! (In truth, that prosecutor, Bruce Hudock, was not an asshole by any definition. He was a very competent prosecutor who was torn between providing my client with a fair trial and delivering some measure of justice to the family of the victim.)

After a day or so, we all became very accustomed to the microphones and the rest of the television trappings. I learned that we could use them to our advantage in some measure. Rather than study my notes from each day's testimony or pay a gazillion dollars to the court reporters for daily transcripts, I convinced the Court TV/CBS people to allow me to look at each day's "dailies." Seeing the testimony for the second time was a real luxury in deciding what points needed to be made in direct- or cross-examination, and most important, in the final argument before the jury. The TV and news people also served as a kind of "shadow jury" for us during that trial. They were trained observers, and I found their input invaluable in determining what aspects of the evidence and testimony were more (or less) effective.

My client was going to testify in this case. This is not only unusual, but pretty much unheard of in a case where an insanity defense is being used. How could I prepare him for the pressure of being cross-examined? I generally sneak into the courthouse with a client during lunch recess or after court has recessed for the day. I put the client in the witness box and allow a friend to conduct a very aggressive cross-examination. This is often quite helpful, but I wanted to try something different in this trial.

Meredith Vieira, having just left *60 Minutes*, was the host of a CBS show called *Verdict*, which was filming the trial along with Court TV. Shortly before my client testified, I allowed Meredith to interview him in her hotel suite, with all of the lights, cameras, and attendant hoopla. This interview was not going to be aired until months after the trial, so I didn't need to worry about any impact the interview might have on the jury. More important, I placed *no* restrictions on any aspect of the interview. If my client could hold up under the grilling of a seasoned and aggressive reporter, under the lights of three cameras, his testimony at the courthouse would be a walk in the park.

He did very well.

I also went to school on this exercise. I stole her questions and used them for the trial. I even tried some of the techniques that had worked so well for her. For instance, she would ask a tough question and my client would answer as best he could. She would then simply stare at him as if he had more to say. There would be a short but awkward moment of silence, only to be broken by my client, adding to his answer. The second response always seemed to bring the best answer. I tried it in court and it worked well for me there. It still does.

As I have said before, I believe that lawyers actually act less dramatically when they are on TV. I was no exception. I did not try to ham it up for the cameras, but rather, made sure that I was more prepared than I had ever been so that my cousins in Yakima would not be embarrassed. I really believe that this is one of the great benefits of televised trials. Another by-product of the televised trial is the absolutely enormous following these trials have generated across the country. In the "big" cases, viewers call in to Court TV and the other stations covering the case with comments and questions that are often incredibly insightful. They discuss the case in chat rooms and message boards on the Internet, and they seem to have a working knowledge of the crime, the witnesses, and the evidence that often surpasses that of the prosecutor and defense counsel alike.

While taking calls one day on Court TV, I talked with a viewer who had called in with an amazingly important question that none of us on TV had thought of (nor did it seem to have occurred to the defense lawyer). During the luncheon recess, I called the defense lawyer in Texas and told him what the viewer had said. He ended up using the question and spending an hour on the issue when court resumed! That is also a measure of the lawyer's skill. We don't know everything, and we should always welcome any suggestion made by anyone who might be able to help us move the ball forward. This is especially true when we get some information or suggestion from someone who is not connected to the case and is thinking outside the box.

Court TV continued to entice the public to enter the courtroom via their living rooms. The Florida rape trial of William Kennedy Smith hooked a substantial number of viewers. Betty Broderick's trial out of San Diego concerned the murder of an ex-husband and his trophy wife by a very embittered and agitated first wife. There was enormous interest in this real-life soap opera—and a lot of rejected first wives rooted for the shooter. We all grew to love and hate the Menendez brothers. (I can never remember which one had the bad rug.)

But finally, like the appearance of the monolith in *2001: A Space Odyssey*, we were all drawn to the television to watch O.J. It was the best of times and it was the worst of times. We could not get enough of this trial and the characters in it. Everyone had his or her own theory.

Everyone had his or her own favorite player. We all loved America's houseguest, Brian "Kato" Kaelin. Everyone learned how you establish time of death: by the sound of barking dogs. Jay Leno had the Dancing Itos on his show. We all loved Mark Fuhrman . . . then we hated Mark Fuhrman . . . and then we didn't know if we should love him or hate him. As it turns out, Mark Fuhrman wrote several well-received books in the years following that trial. While I certainly disagree strongly with the book he wrote advocating the guilt of Michael Skakel, I did appreciate the fact that he wrote a book against the death penalty. Go know.

Other networks went on to produce clones of Court TV, but with a considerable amount of added schmaltz. Geraldo Rivera's 9:00 P.M. *Rivera Live* on CNBC actually became the "show of record" for the O.J. Simpson trial. What does that mean? How did his show get selected? Was there a panel of judges and legal scholars in Washington who made that determination? I used to always ask him that. It still cracks me up. Regardless, everyone watched his show each night, and it was great TV. More important, he is credited with having invented most of today's "legal commentators" (or maybe he should be blamed for it). Either way, he was (and is) a very real person, and it's always a pleasure to work with him.

The Simpson case spawned a virtual generation of TV "big case" trial addicts. Viewers from everywhere and from every demographic became addicted to the trial. They knew minutiae about the case that the real players probably didn't even know—or really care about. Having dealt with the e-mails, telephone call-ins, and street comments and questions of these trial addicts, I was always amazed at their insight into some of the issues, evidence, and witnesses that we geniuses had never considered. In short, this new audience was able to often think outside the box and come up with some incredibly brilliant questions that the lawyers, inside and out of the courtroom, ought to have thought of.

What was so amazing to me was the wide spectrum of people who got hooked on the Simpson trial. This anecdote says it best. I was on vacation in Hawaii with my family. On the first day, we were sitting on lounge chairs by the pool. After a few minutes, the pool guy set up several chairs right near us. My jaw dropped when Academy Award–winning director Barry Levinson and his family were ushered into these chairs, just eight feet away. As I've mentioned, I am a movie buff, and Levinson's credits are amazing: *Bugsy; Good Morning, Vietnam; Diner; Tin Men; Avalon; Wag the Dog; Sleepers; The Natural* . . . He won the Academy Award for directing *Rain Man*. I was dying to meet him, but didn't want to invade his privacy.

After about twenty minutes, my daughter Jamie walked by his chair on her way to get a soda or something. I saw him stop her, and they appeared to be talking about something. She then came over to me as he looked over and smiled. Jamie explained that he was a big fan of Geraldo's show, and he watched me all the time. Would I mind if he came over to talk with me about the case? This is an absolutely true story. (His daughter later shared the fact that the family knew not to disturb him between 9:00 and 10:00 P.M. each night so he could watch Geraldo and my cronies pontificate about the trial.) Barry came over, and we ended up golfing together for the next two weeks. Barry would ask me about the trial, and I would ask him about eight thousand questions about his movies and the movie business.

One day, I thought I would really impress him with my movie knowledge. I told him that I felt there was only one movie that truly depicted the insanity of what really goes on in the courthouse. Did he know which one? He didn't. Smugly, I said it was . . . *And Justice for All*, starring Al Pacino, where the exasperated defense lawyer flips out during his final argument before the jury. Frustrated that his client, a despicable judge who he knows is guilty of rape, is going to beat the case, Pacino declares that the prosecutor "is not gonna get his client today!" Why? Because *he* is! He then proceeds to tell the jury what a scumbag his client is, and that they have to find him guilty. We all remember the signature line of the movie, as the judge (a suicidal nut played by Jack Warden) hollers out, "You're out of order!" Pacino counters with, "No . . . *you're* out of order! We're *all* out of order!" Pleased with myself for educating the Academy Award–winning director, I waited for Barry to tell me whether he'd ever seen this movie that I'd so expertly summarized.

"I wrote it," Barry said.

As the Jack Nicholson character said in *A Few Good Men* after asking how Tom Cruise's dad was doing (only to be told that he was dead): "Well, don't I feel like a fucking asshole!"

Barry Levinson was one of the executive producers for *American Tragedy* (2000), an excellent television miniseries about the O.J. trial. A year or so later, he moved to Connecticut, and we continue to play a lot of golf together. The fact that such a major creative player in the entertainment business could be so interested in the case is simply a testament to the immense public interest in today's big cases.

This encounter and newfound friendship with Barry Levinson resulted in the fulfillment of one of my lifetime goals. (No, not to argue before the Supreme Court.) Barry wrote me into one of his movies! In *Man of the Year*, starring Robin Williams, Christopher Walken, Laura Linney, and others, I play "Talking Head Lawyer." In one scene I appear on Laura Linney's bathroom television set, pontificating about Robin Williams's election to the presidency. My friends and family have had to suffer through countless obnoxious instances where I've let my SAG card fall out of my wallet so people can ask me what it is.

• • •

Budding film career aside, waiting for a verdict is an incredibly nerve-wracking experience that generally makes every lawyer perpetually nauseous throughout the entire process. We have nothing left to do for the case. It is out of our hands. We just wait for that knock on the door to the deliberation room. As we sat in front of various cameras in our little tents and in studios around the country, waiting for the

Peterson verdict, we all tried to guess what the jury was thinking about this or that. Catherine Crier, on Court TV, asked me why the jury was taking so long. I expressed my opinion that the jury was afraid to come out of the building after returning the verdict, and having to face the "frenzied mob!"

"You really think they are afraid of the crowd outside?" asked Catherine.

"No; the crowd is no problem," I said. "I'm talking about the morning-show bookers!"

Like I said, waiting for a jury gets us a bit crazy.

When the death penalty verdict for Peterson was being announced, I was in a studio at NBC in New York City, doing commentary for MSNBC. After they announced that the jury had reached a verdict, the networks had about a half hour to gear up. I asked my cameraperson if any of the major networks were broadcasting this verdict, or if it was just the cable news people. She looked at her bank of monitors and kind of screamed, "Oh my God—they're even cutting into *Oprah!*" I guess it doesn't get any bigger than that.

Not only do the big cases generate viewer interest, but they can even prompt people to actually get involved. While waiting outside the Scott Peterson courtroom one morning, I was greeted by a very nice woman who introduced herself as Jordy, from Phoenix. She, together with a few others from around the country, were all friends from the Court TV Internet Message Board. They had all traveled to California to watch the trial. Like Beth Karas, senior reporter for Court TV, there was little they did not know about every aspect of the case. They invited me to join them over the weekend for an excursion out into the San Francisco Bay. They had rented a boat and some dredging equipment, and planned to go out with an engineer to try and find the missing anchors. I thanked them but declined. I asked Jordy if she believed Peterson was guilty, and she very calmly and professionally recapped all the damning evidence against him. Her presentation was better than 85 percent of the prosecutors I have ever seen in court.

While such an idea may sound absurd on its face—a trial observer becoming an expert—you never really know. After the Sharon Tate murders in Los Angeles, the police had taken a statement from one of the Manson women who described the grisly murders, and then, how they had driven off, throwing the bloody clothes out the window of their car. After that statement was made public, a reporter closely followed the statement in terms of what roads were taken, for how long, etc. They stopped at a certain place, looked over the embankment, and found all the bloody evidence right there!

• • •

So now that we've covered the positives of the O.J. trial—the spawning of big-case trial addicts; educating the public about the justice system, and thereby creating legal experts from amateurs; and encouraging viewers to think outside the box—what exactly were the negatives? Most people thought (and still believe) that O.J. is guilty but got away with it. They blame the system. They blame the lawyers. And they blame the process. They feel that the judge lost control of the case and it became a circus. They believe that this all happened because everyone acts like a schmuck when there are cameras on them.

So what happened after that trial? Judges across the country said no to cameras in their courts, saying they "did not want to become another Ito." I have always felt that this was a bad rap for everyone. I really do not believe that any of the lawyers or players in that case would have acted very differently had there been no cameras in the courtroom. Could Judge Ito have done a better job? Maybe; maybe not. But using this case as an excuse to stop televising trials around the country was wrong.

When Court TV started, there were major concerns about some aspects of having cameras in the courtroom. A major worry was that certain witnesses would not show up if the case was being televised. Presumably, they would not want the world to see them testifying about their having had that affair or whatever. Nothing could have been further from the reality of what happened. Over the years, we have seen that the most despicable and humiliated people will show up to testify in these cases, wearing their best polyester suits. The prospect of being on TV seems to totally cancel out any thought that maybe they are going to look like a real schmuck in front of the viewing public.

Like any great spectacle, the big case does seem to bring out the Big Nuts. If you watched any of the Peterson trial, you invariably saw a guy named Frank pacing around with his sign behind pretty much anyone and everyone who was on camera. His sign read:

KENNERLY

12 GALAXIES

PSYCHROZUTICUL TECHNOLOGIST

CBS: LELDTROKONIKAL COVERAGE

ZORKIRUTICUL

DECOROUS STEELY

REMINISCENCE

I asked him what the sign meant, and he very politely explained how it had something to do with the upcoming collision of galaxies, global warming, and the Dixie Chicks. (Okay, I admit to throwing in the Dixie Chicks part to make it funnier.) After I was on camera for some show, Frank asked me whom I was reporting for. Not to be outdone, I explained that I was reporting on the trial for my home planet, Gorkon, located in a nearby galaxy. "The Gorkonites are really into this trial!" I said. He was thrilled to hear this, and we exchanged cards.

Recent high-profile cases have shown the early (and subsequent) critics of televised trials that it can work without great discomfort, cost, or embarrassment to the community hosting the trial. If you can't beat them, hire them to run the show. This was the obvious decision made by the powers-that-be in Redwood City, California, when they realized that the broadcast personalities and their producers were there to stay. After the TV people balked at paying the big bucks, relations deteriorated between the media hordes and the city, court administration, and sheriff's department. In their defense, these agencies and departments had no prior experience with handling such logistics problems. Moreover, there is a great deal of inherent mistrust and wariness on the part of court employees. These reporters and their producers were not there to make sure things ran smoothly in the world of the courthouse. They are a traveling circus of aggressive, nosy people who just want to invade the courthouse to get a story! They have no stake in the community and can be tough to deal with; give them an inch, they want three feet.

"It's a pageant!" That was what Dustin Hoffman's character (an extravagant movie producer supposedly modeled after Paramount's Robert Evans) declared in Barry Levinson's classic film *Wag the Dog*. The president needed someone to "produce" a war as a distraction, to deflect media attention away from his sexual encounter with a young girl. Using the same genius, the major networks at the Peterson trial got together and decided they needed a producer—someone who could handle *all* the media characters and somehow work things out with all the city agencies in charge of this criminal trial.

They found Peter Shaplen, a veteran television producer with an uncanny knack for juggling a lot of difficult people with very large egos. In an incredible coup for most everyone, the Redwood City officials bought into this idea and delegated an enormous amount of authority to Shaplen. He decided who got credentials, courtroom seats, and so on. He would hear the demands of the journalists, producers, and everyone else, and then successfully negotiate with the court and sheriff's people. How many cameras would be inside the hallway? Where would the principals be "shot" as they came and went from the courthouse, and on and on. Would any parts of the trial be televised live? Where would there be an overflow "listening room" for those journalists who didn't get a pass for inside the courtroom? How would members of the public get passes?

I spoke to Peter many times out there and never ceased to be amazed by the wisdom of the media and city officials in letting a professional producer "produce" a murder trial. (Not surprisingly, Peter would later assume the same role in the Michael Jackson trial.) Some of the scenes from the Peterson trial could have come from the movie *Network*! I did get a kick out of the press passes, though. I think the sheriff's office got a little out of hand in making sure we all knew these passes were for the "Peterson Trial Only!" (Did they think Dan Abrams or Geraldo would use them to sneak into the Epstein divorce trial or the Smith eviction hearing?)

Of course, the most common post-O.J. argument against televised trials is that the lawyers are going to act up for the cameras. As mentioned before, I have tried a case on Court TV, and over the past fourteen years, I have appeared as a trial commentator at least every other week. My experience is that the lawyers actually tone it down when they know the cameras are on. Very simply put, we don't want to look like jerks on national television! But most important, the cameras have the best impact on the judges. Only once have I seen a judge act really stupid or abusive during a televised trial. Generally, a judge in these cases will be extra cautious about his or her demeanor, and even more so, his rulings. This can only be a good thing.

The only valid argument against the cameras is the exposure of a rape victim or a child's identity. This is not an unsolvable problem. When televised trials first began, they put a blue screen over the victim's face (as in the William Kennedy Smith case). It worked fine. I really believe the system works better when we are watching it. The public has the right to see and understand what is going on in the courtroom; they are *public* courtrooms, after all.

Sometimes, the cameras can also serve the public good in other ways. In 2001, a black man named Amadou Diallo was confronted by some New York City police officers outside of his apartment. They mistakenly believed he was a dangerous individual about whom they had received a call. Diallo made a "furtive" gesture, which an officer mistakenly believed to be a move for a weapon. An officer close to him stumbled, and all hell broke loose. In a few minutes, Diallo lay dead, with forty-one bullets in him from the guns of four police officers. The New York City community, black and white, was outraged. Bruce Springsteen wrote and performed a song damning the police, called "41 Shots." The officers were charged with the killing. Their trial was moved from New York City to upstate Albany, New York. They would certainly be convicted. How could they shoot this man forty-one times? They were obviously bigoted animals, out of control.

The case was televised. We watched the officers testify. We watched them cry. We saw how they were totally inexperienced and had never worked together or really knew what to expect. They screwed up—but they were not the demons we had expected them to be. The jury found them not guilty. Were they responsible? Of course. But the jury did not think they were criminals. What really mattered most, in my opinion, was the public's reaction to that verdict. There were no significant protests or incidents of civil unrest. The community, regardless of color, saw the trial and accepted the verdict. If that verdict had been delivered from behind closed doors, I do not believe there would have been such acceptance of the case's resolution. It's pretty basic: We are always better off seeing what is happening ourselves than having someone tell us what they think is important for us to know. The jury is still out on allowing cameras in the courtrooms. Hopefully, the judges will shake that Ito-phobia thing soon.

• • •

Can the high-profile defendant get a fair trial? I am not sure. Where the playing field is fairly level, it should occur. Where there is a wide disparity between the "in" court and "out" of court skills of the lawyers, it may not happen. Someone once put it simply: A trial is a contest between two sides as to who can get the best lawyer. Today's definition of "the best lawyer" now includes their talents in front of the cameras or a bank of microphones, in addition to their courtroom skills. In the end, it is ultimately the responsibility of the judge to ensure that a fair trial is received by all concerned. The judge must balance the competitive interests of the defendant's right to a fair trial versus the intense efforts by the media to learn and report every detail of the case, which often may prejudice the defense or the prosecution.

The media always wants the judge to release the arrest warrants, search warrants, and accompanying affidavits, which are often the subject of considerable pretrial motions and hearings. They contain all the information that the police and the prosecution have dug up on the accused, which provided a judge with enough cause in the first place to order the person arrested or his property searched or seized. These are not balanced accounts of the alleged misconduct or the police investigations. They generally are one-sided versions of what the prosecution believes happened and why the accused is probably guilty. There is virtually no input from the defense. By their very nature, these are documents designed to persuade the reader that the guy is guilty!

In the big cases, the media can't wait to subject these documents to a microanalysis, since they contain all the juicy stuff: blood, semen, guns, confessions, jailhouse rats, and more. The problem is, there's generally some kind of gag order in effect that does not allow the defense to comment on these accusations once they have become fodder for the nightly news or the Internet. Only one side is ever going to come out, and that's not fair. Recognizing this, the judges do their best to keep them under seal. Of course, the defense is constantly being roasted as trying to hide the ball when this happens. This is where the judge has to earn his or her salary. They have to have the courage to take the hit in the media for being secretive in order to take their best shot in giving the accused a fair trial. That old balancing act again.

The big case *can* produce a fair trial. The judges need only to remember not to waste their energy by worrying about "becoming another Ito," and to not fall into a siege mentality with the media. The media can be an enormous distraction and can certainly ratchet up the degree of difficulty judges experience in doing their jobs. But they are not the enemy.

A new breed of court employees has been spawned from these cases—court information officers, press clerks, media officers, and so on. These are people who are learning to deal with the issues that have been born out of the high-profile trial. Where should they park the satellite trucks? Does the local weekly, free, left-wing newspaper get a seat in the courtroom next to *The New York Times*? If NBC has five sets of producers there for five different shows, do they get five seats? Where can the defendant and his lawyer, family, bodyguard, and family spokesperson park without having to walk through the gauntlet of media? Which door can the accused and the victim's entourages enter and exit each day without going through a similar gauntlet? Does the defense get a room to keep their files in each night, or do they have to haul them all into the courthouse each day, like Sherpa bearers making their way to Camp Three? If copies of documents are made for the press, who gets them first?

The smart court systems have learned to work with the 800-pound gorilla instead of making believe it is not there, or that it might be going away anytime soon. They can learn the lesson from Redwood City about being too greedy. One commentator made a very logical suggestion that there be "high-profile media" insurance for municipalities. Some enterprising insurance guy should be all over that idea!

One of the very advanced and incredibly convenient things I appreciated about Judge Delucchi's courtroom in the Peterson case was the fact that it was WiFi. For a very reasonable fee, you could sit in the trial with your laptop connected to the Internet—and to your producer in the tent down the street, or the studio in New York. As the witnesses would testify, you could hear a steady and soft cacophony of everyone typing. When a witness would mention the name of an expert, sixty people would immediately Google the name and relay the information to their producers or reporters, also sitting with their laptops or BlackBerries. This allowed reporters like Court TV's Beth Karas to sit in front of a camera a block away with one eye on the camera and the other on her BlackBerry, telling us what was happening that very minute. Beth is very much like the most devoted and informed Trekkie at a Star Trek convention. There is no amount of Peterson trial minutiae she does not know! What is even more amazing is the fact that she would share her information with other journalists, despite the extraordinarily fierce competition that exists between journalists to get "something that nobody else has."

One morning, one of the Fox News producers made the mistake of asking me to feed them what was going on in the courtroom with my laptop. Nora Zimmett is a classic aggressive yet amiable producer who takes her job very seriously and is totally concerned with both getting it right along with getting it first. I told her I would e-mail or instant-message anything significant during the morning session. My first message was: "This is unbelievable—Peterson just punched out Geragos and has lunged over the counsel table and has Judge Delucchi in a headlock! It's pandemonium in here!" This was followed by: "Incredible! Robert Blake just burst into the courtroom and confessed to killing Laci!" Fairly soon after that, Nora sent someone else into the courtroom to feed the information to her.

So what is the bottom line with these high-profile cases? Are they destined to be perverted spectacles whereby the unfortunate schmuck on trial is doomed? I honestly don't think so. Communities across the country have learned a lot about the nature of the beast, and how to work *with* the media instead of against it. However, the key element will always be the person with the robe. The judge in the big case needs only a sense of basic fairness, a lot of common sense, and some patience in dealing with these people and the issues that come along with them. It can be done.

One interesting by-product of the public's exposure to celebrity cases such as O.J. Simpson's has been a somewhat unrealistic expectation of a criminal trial. Howard Ehring, a seasoned public defender in Stamford, Connecticut, is used to hearing his new clients say amusing things, reflecting some naivete about the system. I am not referring to court-house fractured words, which I kind of collect. ("Are you my Public *Offender*? Are you gonna speak to the *prostitutor* and get me a *flea* bar-gain? Do I need to *detain* a real lawyer?"). Shortly after the Simpson case, Ehring was appointed to represent a young man charged with some minor theft. When he walked into the interrogation room to meet his new client, the young man looked over Ehring's shoulder in disbelief and frustration. "Hey, man—where's the rest of my team?"

{Chapter 10}

Losing
the Case:
From Savior to Shithead
without Passing Go

LOSING REALLY SUCKS. There are simply no better words to describe this experience. All your effort, sweat, and dedication to this client and his case have meant *nothing*. We have failed to protect him from the life-changing disaster that a conviction visits upon the client and his family.

A close friend and seasoned criminal defense lawyer from my town, Bob Bello, once represented a man who was charged with murdering a woman as she walked to her car in the Bloomingdale's parking lot. Nobody wanted this case, and the public defenders were overjoyed when Bob volunteered to take the case pro bono. So not only was he going to defend this very unpopular accused, but he also wasn't going to earn a penny for it. In point of fact, he would probably lose some business from clients who were pissed off that Bob would defend this despicable person. It was a very sad crime in our relatively sleepy town, and the community rejoiced when the jury returned a guilty verdict. I had seen much of the trial, and Bob had done a great job with very little to work with. I walked over to tell him so, and that he should hold his head high. Crestfallen, he thanked me, but added, "Let's face it—a second-year law student could have gotten the same result." That really sums it up best. He was inconsolable.

A week later, I was involved in some very high-profile case, and *Time* magazine was coming to interview me at my office. I called Bob, who was still smarting from the Bloomingdale's murder loss. I left him a message that it was very important he call me back between 1:00 and 2:00 that afternoon. When he called at about 1:15, I told him I couldn't speak to him right then because *Time* magazine people were there, interviewing me. He said he would call back later in the afternoon. I told him that wasn't necessary. Puzzled, he asked me why I wanted him to call me. I explained that I'd just wanted to be able to tell him that I couldn't talk to him because *Time* magazine was interviewing me. This was my way of consoling him. He got the joke. A good sport, he was accustomed to and appreciative of my sick sense of humor.

We don't get credit for *trying* really hard, nor should we. We have been hired to do a specific job, and when we lose, it's because we didn't produce. Green Bay Packer icon Vince Lombardi said it best: "Winning isn't everything . . . it's the *only* thing!" While this might not be the best credo for Little League coaches to drill into the fragile minds of thirteen-year-old kids, it *does* accurately describe the mission of the criminal defense lawyer.

Many people think that we don't like to lose because it is a blow to our ego. Sometimes you see lawyers on TV who are introduced as someone who "never lost a case." There is a Latin term for those people: BULLSHITTERS! Okay, it isn't Latin—but it is the truth. Anyone who is in the business of defending people accused of serious crimes will lose some cases during their career. It's just the nature of the beast. The prosecutors are generally not going to try crappy cases. Those will be plea-bargained away. That is one of the luxuries of being a prosecutor. On the contrary, we defense lawyers must try the difficult cases. They are the ones that won't go away quietly. There is generally a good reason why the prosecutor doesn't throw the case out or offer some lesser plea deal. They feel they have a strong case, or the crime (or the alleged criminal) is so significant that they will let the jury decide.

Criminal defense lawyers don't care about win/loss records. I realize that such a statement sounds like absolute baloney, but I really believe that the great majority of criminal defense lawyers care about delivering the best result for our clients, period. Obviously, losing cases does not promote that end. My real point is simple: *It is not about us!* It is about the client. Is a guilty verdict a blow to our egos? Of course. But that blow is a pinprick compared to the intense pain we feel in our gut when we lose a case.

It is no secret that I passionately believe Michael Skakel is totally innocent of the crime for which he was found guilty. I will never believe that he had anything to do with the murder of Martha Moxley. His case is still being appealed, and I have no intention of discussing the merits of the case or how wrong I believe the jury was. What I can say is that I have not slept a full night since the day the jury came in with their verdict. I am probably singularly responsible for the increase in stockholder dividends in Ambien. Everyone told me that I did a great job. Strangers and lawyers around the country sent me very supportive letters. I only heard and continue to replay Bob Bello's comment to me: *A second-year law student could have gotten the same result.* I let my client down. I was hired to win, and I lost. At the time of this writing, Michael is still in jail.

Losing a big case in the media is an interesting phenomenon. We saw it happen to Mark Geragos in the Peterson trial, and it certainly happened to me as well. When the case is going well, we are touted as geniuses. Jeffrey Toobin, now of CNN, called me "brilliant" on *Good Morning America.* The media sang my praises up until the moment the jury foreperson uttered the word *guilty.* From that moment on, the entire media mob covering that case essentially pronounced me a schmuck—and further, that evaluation was retroactive. I had always been a schmuck!

Hurtful? Of course it is, but really, nothing compared to the horror of watching my client being handcuffed and taken away because *I lost.* I didn't lose for me . . . I lost for him! It is not about me, but I was in charge of ensuring that his life would not be destroyed. The media "piling on" is just a part of doing the big case. I honestly cared less what they said after that disastrous moment. They are just doing their jobs, and it really doesn't mean much to the defense lawyer in the long run. When we lose, it hurts us. It doesn't hurt because we are afraid of losing clients or being labeled a "loser." It hurts because we have failed our client. This is true regardless of whether it is a local shoplifting charge or a high-profile celebrity case. The sick feeling in our gut is the same. Oddly enough, losing the high-profile case is not the public relations professional disaster that folks may think it is. Unless we fell asleep during the trial or did something really stupid, like having someone try on a glove, the public doesn't really seem to drop us down too many notches, even when we lose and get hammered in the press.

After both the guilt phase and the penalty phase of the Scott Peterson trial, Mark Geragos took a severe beating in the media. I saw him try the case from the courtroom. He was well prepared, and he did a damn good job of taking apart the State's case. Where he ran into problems was with his own witnesses. They were not as strong as one would like them to be. More important, the facts of the case were not so great for the defense. Geragos had no control over Peterson having given his fishing alibi, which placed him at the exact spot where the bodies were eventually recovered.

Sometime near the middle of the Peterson trial, I sat down with Mark Geragos for some coffee back at the hotel where we were all staying. He was quite calm and collected. Having done "the big case," I understand and appreciate the adrenaline rush that takes over your entire nervous system, allowing you to basically spend twenty-four hours a day on the edge of your seat, waiting for the next witness, crisis, or ruling. I did not "interview" Mark. We commiserated about the inherent difficulty of representing someone whom a great many people dislike, and how the jury can transfer that emotion to the lawyer. Not really jokingly, Mark commented, "One of the jurors wants to vaporize me." It's not that we tend to get paranoid, but it can be a bit tough trying to make a point to a juror who looks at you as if you just stole his grandmother's purse!

Mark Geragos told me he truly believes Scott Peterson is innocent. The jury and most of the English-speaking world may disagree with Mark, but I honestly think that Mark believed in his client's innocence. The public in general believes that criminal defense lawyers, especially high-profile ones, are largely full of crap and will take anyone's case and declare them innocent to the world in exchange for a boatload of money. It is assumed that we always say we believe our clients are innocent, but we're really just posing. It's kind of a spin-off from the boy who cried wolf. More like the lawyer who cried "innocent"!

Such a genuine—if not always correct—belief in your client's innocence can be both a blessing and a curse. On the good side, if you truly believe in your client, that emotion may be observed and appreciated by the public, and more important, the jury. This counts for something. Leslie Abramson, the tenacious California attorney who tried (and embraced) the Menendez brothers, totally conveyed to the world that she *believed* in these boys. Nobody else did, but it was abundantly clear that she was convinced they were innocent. I believe she was able to keep the first Menendez jury from convicting them because of the jury's perception of her unswerving belief in them.

On the other hand, if you lose the case, you feel you have been part of an out-of-control machine that has screwed someone who should not be in jail. It really makes no difference that you did your best; you were driving the bus when it crashed and that's all that matters—to everyone.

Geragos did convey, at least to me, that he believes Scott Peterson is innocent. Did the jury see that? Did they care? Apparently not. A defense attorney can only do so much. We are dealt certain cards and have to play that hand. When we win, we are heroes. When we lose, we are schmucks.

Linda Deutsch of the Associated Press wrote a very critical piece after the Peterson trial, titled LEGAL HOTSHOT'S STAR HAS FALLEN. Essentially echoing my reasoning that the public believes Geragos is a jerk since he lost the case, she interviewed Leslie Abramson. I have always told lawyers to beware of taking the high-profile case, because if you live on the front page, you can also die on the front page. Abramson said it better in the AP piece. Explaining that this case will not be the end of Geragos, she said: "Once your name's out there, it's out there . . . . Mark doesn't care about money, but he did care about fame. Sometimes when you pursue that beast, it eats you!"

Leslie Abramson's comment about Geragos not really being professionally hurt because "his name is out there," illustrates the odd fact that people don't fault you for losing the big case. What seems to be more important than winning (or not losing) is that you are in the game at the highest level. I certainly don't agree with this logic, but it seems that I am in the minority.

Being somewhat famous for having lost a big case, I can confirm the public's obsession with the high-profile case and the sometimes-odd reaction to my having lost.

"You never expected to win, did you?"

"Why did you lose?"

"I forgot—did you win or lose that case?"

"Did you still get paid even though you lost?"

"How did it feel to lose?"

My most memorable and painful street encounter was about two years after the Skakel verdict. I was walking across 57th Street in New York City on a busy afternoon. As I was about midway across, together with the typical mob of strangers all hurrying to wherever, a lady coming toward me suddenly looked at me like I was Josef Mengele Jr. Without breaking stride, she simply said, "How did you lose that case?" Before I could even consider answering, she was well on her way to Bergdorf's (or her Communist cell meeting).

What really does matter after a loss is the deterioration that occurs between the lawyer and the client. I have not lost very many cases, but when it has happened, the end result is pretty much the same. Up to the moment of the verdict, the client and his or her family have nothing but praise, admiration, and unswerving support for my efforts. I am nothing less than a genius in the courtroom. I get credit for engineering every little subtle victory as I destroy the State's witness or make some other point in our favor. As we wait for the verdict, I am told, "Mickey, we just want you to know that no matter what happens, we think you did a great job, and we will always appreciate everything you've done."

Cut to the jury foreperson somberly saying that horrible "G" word. The client and the family (and myself as well) are generally in shock. The client is immediately handcuffed, and everyone is crying. The client's family, friends, and clergy are crying in torment, while the victim's family is crying for their own reasons: closure, retribution, the deliverance of "justice." I tell the client and his family that we will do everything possible to right this wrong. We will get the best appeal lawyers. We will try and get the judge to allow bond while the appeal is pending. We all walk out of the courtroom and the building like zombies.

From that moment on I am no longer their champion. I am someone who fucked up! During the appeal process, I may often become the target or basis for their appeal. Most appellate lawyers will do everything (as well they should) to find some basis for a new trial. Sooner or later, they will zero in on the trial lawyer's "ineffectiveness." It is the way the system works, and the criminal defense lawyer is supposed to appreciate it and not take it personally. Easier said than done. In the end, all that counts is what happens to the client.

I certainly do not fault my client or his family for appearing "ungrateful" for my efforts. They are the ones who have become the losers here. If they make a disparaging remark about my performance,

I can only take the hit and move forward. I am going to be able to go home to my family. My client does not—and may never—have that freedom again. The criminal defense lawyer learns to understand and appreciate their anger and frustration. If we can't live with it, we should be doing some other kind of law.

Chapter 11

Undefendable?

The Story of Roger Ligon

ON A VERY HOT DAY in August 1989, Roger Ligon was walking the grounds of the housing development in Stamford, Connecticut, where he lived with his wife and two young daughters. Forty-two years old, he suffered from a heart disability, yet worked part-time as the maintenance man for the apartment complex. Willie Dobson pulled into a parking space in the complex. This was his twenty-second birthday. Roger asked him to move his car because he was in a no-parking area next to a fire hydrant. Rules are rules. Willie's mother, who lived in the complex, got involved and started hollering at Roger. Roger held his ground and insisted that the car be moved. There had been a minor fire recently and the fire truck had had problems getting close enough to the hydrant. Willie had a hot temper and lost his patience very quickly. "You're doomed. I'm coming back with my boys . . . You're a dead man."

Roger removed a gun from his belt and fired three times, hitting Willie twice. "Please don't kill me!" Willie begged. Roger fired the fourth shot into his head, ending his life. Willie's mother and other neighbors watched in horror. Roger walked back to his apartment, called the police, and waited to be arrested. He kept his door wide open and sat at a table with the gun clearly on it, in full view of anyone entering the apartment. He wanted to make sure the police could see him and that the gun was not in his hands when they approached. He confessed to the detectives on videotape and was presented in court the following morning.

I was contacted by his cardiologist, as well as several other people who knew Roger. Would I defend him? He was "a terrific guy" and "really didn't belong in jail." I had read the headline in the paper: MAN SHOT DEAD IN AN ARGUMENT OVER PARKING SPOT. I didn't want to get involved. Obviously this was one of those "misdemeanor murders"— one bad guy killing another. I often questioned myself later on whether I felt this way because both men were black. Could I have been that shallow, prejudiced, or jaded? I had actually represented the victim in this case earlier, for some serious charges.

A few weeks went by. I couldn't help but notice Roger at the courthouse. I would see him with his public defender as I was taking care of other cases of mine. There really was something about him that did not compute. He seemed to have this very quiet and respectful dignity about him that is generally absent in the courtroom—lawyers included! He appeared neither bitter nor angry about his plight, but seemed to dutifully accept his future as it would be dictated by the criminal justice system.

I agreed to speak to his boss from the apartment complex. She came to my office and tearfully explained how Roger was the best worker she had ever had, and one of the best people she had ever known. This was the same story I heard from the cardiologist, a real estate lawyer, and many others who had called me about Roger. I had obviously prejudged him and the case based on my cynicism from having spent too many years listening to too many bullshit stories from too many clients. All these people could not be wrong.

I spoke to the public defender, social worker, and investigator handling the case. I looked at the police reports and the transcript of his confession. I sat down with Roger and his family. One of eight children, he had dropped out of school in the fifth grade in Montgomery, Alabama, to help support his family. He moved to Stamford, Connecticut, at age twelve, getting a job as a dishwasher. He joined the U.S. Marines at eighteen and went through Parris Island twice. (He was a bit overweight the first time, and agreed to do it again!) He was a devoted husband and father, insisting on driving both his children and his wife to school and work every day to make sure they were safe.

He was admired and respected by everyone in the community; well, not everyone. He *had* made some enemies. Whenever he saw someone buying or selling drugs, he immediately called the narcotics squad and directed them to the sellers, buyers, or the stash itself. He hadn't done this anonymously. He would proudly stand by and wait for the police to arrive. He was not afraid of these people. He wasn't a vigilante—just a damn good citizen. So why does such a good person do such an incredibly bad thing? I believed that the answer had something to do with Vietnam. In the course of his videotaped confession, the very seasoned homicide detective asked Roger, almost out of nowhere, if he had served in Vietnam. The answer was yes. Roger had served in Vietnam as a marine, and had been wounded and later, decorated. But the better question was why the detective had even asked the question. He obviously saw or sensed something that might be the key to this tragedy.

Roger had been interviewed by the social worker and investigator for the public defender, both of whom had made similar inquiries about Vietnam. Roger had related that his life had really changed over there. He went through some very bad experiences that left him unable to sleep. He would get up in the middle of the night and patrol the apartment, checking the doors and windows. I learned later that this is called "hypervigilant behavior." He needed alcohol to fall asleep. He did not go out to bars or become disorderly in any way. He just could not sleep without medicating himself in some fashion. This alcohol intake had damaged his heart, and that is how he came to know my cardiologist friend.

I had attended a criminal law seminar a few years earlier where someone a lot smarter than me lectured about the defense of posttraumatic stress disorder (PTSD). It was not an easy defense to use.

You had to prove that the accused had experienced some extraordinary event that somehow related to the crime he committed years later. Airline disasters, car crashes, rapes, and other such traumatic experiences often left their victims with PTSD. Military experiences were more difficult to deal with in this defense because it was very hard to prove that the "stressor" event had occurred years earlier. Veterans' faded memories are sometimes exaggerated and nearly impossible to document, often leaving juries skeptical of the defense.

Roger had told the social worker about a few incidents that seemed to justify the PTSD defense. Looking at the social worker's notes, I found three specific incidents Roger had described that would probably satisfy the definition of such a stressor. One incident involved a firefight his Marine Corps unit was involved in, where his close friend JoJo had been incinerated by napalm right in front of him. Roger had tried to retrieve his friend's body. He grabbed JoJo's arm, but the flesh tore off the bone. He still had nightmares about the incident, and it bothered him to no end. How do you prove this happened? And if it did, how does it excuse Roger's conduct in killing Dobson? Most important, would a jury buy this? Would anyone?

Roger generally did not remember the last names of any of the men he had served with twenty years earlier. They were all known by nicknames, which I learned was common in a combat unit. In fact, I learned a lot. I read everything I could find about the PTSD defense and its use in Vietnam cases. It was almost always unsuccessful. Rarely could you prove that the veteran actually went through the traumatic event. That seemed to be the key.

I spent a week in Washington, D.C., at the Marine Corps Historical Center in the Washington Navy Yard. In a small cubbyhole, I was provided with the daily "combat chronologies" written by the commanding officer of each company. I knew Roger was in Kilo Company with the 3rd Battalion, 7th Marines. I knew when he served and when he was wounded. That was about it. These chronologies were not copies; they were the original typed pages, pecked out on a field unit typewriter by a young lieutenant in some hellhole, twenty-two years earlier. They did not contain the names of the soldiers—just how many men were killed or injured, as well as the same statistics for the enemy. I found what appeared to be confirmation of Roger's experiences. I had the dates and the locations of the incidents he had described, which could possibly establish PTSD. They were incredibly close to his descriptions of the events; the only things missing were witnesses.

I drove to the Marine Corps headquarters in Quantico, Virginia, and explained to the records clerk what I was looking for. He politely told me that he was not allowed to give me addresses for the men in any Marine Corps company. They had privacy regulations or something like that. I came back a few hours later and did some serious begging and groveling. I explained Roger's situation and how he had been there for the Marine Corps; now, they needed to be there for him. The clerk met me halfway. He gave me the names of everyone in Roger's unit together with their hometowns from twenty-two years ago. The rest was up to me.

Fair enough. For the next few weeks, we called everyone with these names in towns and cities across the country. I found many of the men Roger had served with. Their reaction to my phone call was always the same. They would pause for a very long time and then cry (or sob) as they related their experiences. It was an amazing phenomenon. As I called these men from the past, I was opening doors that they believed had been slammed shut long ago.

One veteran told me something that was truly amazing. When I asked him about the JoJo incident, he calmly told me that he wasn't at that firefight, but "it was all in the book." Book? What book? He told me that there had been a book written about the 1969 summer offensive of Roger's battalion, and the incident involving JoJo was mentioned in it. Through the Library of Congress, I found the book, which was already out of print. *Death Valley* was published in 1987 by a young Missouri man named Keith Nolan. He had researched the events exhaustively by interviewing hundreds of veterans and sifting through volumes of materials and combat records. On page 296, I found the story. More important, it also led me to the men who could tell the story to the jury. We were ready for trial.

This case had now become close to an obsession for me. I had gotten to know Roger and his family quite well. I now understood how such a good man could have done what he did. If I could not convince a jury of this, his life would be ruined. The more I worked on the case, the more personal it became. Roger and I were about the same age. I had lucked out and flunked the physical for Vietnam, while the Roger Ligons of the world had volunteered to suffer the horrors there. Along the way, they became scarred for life, both inside and out.

A few weeks before jury selection for Roger's case, I was told that the prosecutors had agreed to let Court TV and CBS televise the case. As discussed earlier, Court TV had not yet been launched in the late 1980s, but the producers were already looking for cases to air in the first few months of their operation. The trial would be taped and then aired at a later date. CBS had a new show coming on the air called *Verdict*. Hosted by Meredith Vieira, they would follow a trial and then condense it to a half-hour show. Why would the prosecution agree to this? It was very unlike them. The answer was obvious: They knew about my PTSD defense and figured this would be a slam-dunk win. Why not share their glee with the viewing public? It certainly occurred to me that they might be right.

Selecting the jury was an interesting and unconventional experience. I told the prospective jurors that my client had indeed killed Dobson, who was unarmed at the time. I told them that my defense was PTSD. I was going to ask them to find that my client was technically insane at the time of the killing by reason of things that had happened twenty-two years earlier in Southeast Asia. I asked them if they thought I was crazy! I really did ask that, and many thought I was. But there were many who said that they could keep an open mind. We were able to select a jury that I thought would give Roger a fair shake.

The State's case took just a couple of days. Eyewitnesses, cops, video of the confession, medical examiner—that was about it. Slam dunk? It sure looked like it. Well, maybe not. One of the State's first witnesses was Jesse Ruffin, a longtime friend of the victim and his family. He testified that Willie Dobson was "a nice, easygoing guy." He told the jury how he had watched Roger shoot Willie and then chase him into the parking area where Roger had put a final shot into Willie's head. The witness testified that Willie had shouted, "Don't shoot—please!" as Roger chased him around the car. "There was so much blood, you know, there. And he shot him again and he hit him," said the witness.

When the State finished with him, I knew there was nothing to be gained in trying to shake his eyewitness account of Roger shooting an unarmed man who was begging for his life. That would certainly have been the conventional approach in defending Roger, but this was not the conventional case. Our defense "gave away" these bad facts. The mission was to give the jury a plausible reason for such horrendous behavior. Mr. Ruffin had testified that he was a veteran of Korea. Just maybe I could get him to help me build that bridge from Vietnam to Stamford.

Q: *At the very end of this tragedy, when Roger fired that final shot, you saw Roger as he walked by, right?*
A: Yes.

Q: *In fact, you asked him, "Why did you do that?"*
A: Yes.

Q: *What did Roger say?*
A: He didn't say anything.

Q: *Did he answer you?*
A: No, he didn't.

Q: *Do you think he heard you?*
A: Yes, sir, I think he did.

Q: *Was he running?*
A: No, he walked.

Q: *Walking slowly?*
A: Well, his normal walk.

Q: *Normal walk. Had the gun in his hand?*
A: Yes, sir.

Q: *And he heard you but he didn't answer?*
A: Right.

Q: *And he knows you?*
A: Yes, sir.

Q: *Did he threaten you?*
A: No, he didn't.

Q: *Did you ever see anybody look like that before?*
A: Yes, I seen a lot of people look like that.

Q: *When?*
A: When I was overseas.

Q: *Overseas?*
A: Yes.

Q: *In Korea?*
A: Yes.

Q: *Nothing further.*
Redirect by Prosecutor: Nothing further.

The State's witness, Mr. Ruffin, accurately described "the thousand-yard stare" that would later be explained by the psychiatrists and psychologists as a common phenomenon suffered by combat veterans. It was a good beginning, especially coming from a hostile witness during the State's side of the case. The state's next witness was one of the responding police officers. Detective Corsello, of the major crimes division, described the gruesome crime scene. My job was to ignore that testimony and make him our witness, for our purposes.

The prosecutor had effectively asked the detective if he had examined the body of Willie Dobson and had, in fact, found no weapon. Roger had killed an unarmed man. I took a different tack. The cross-examination opened as follows:

Q: *You were looking for a weapon on Willie Dobson?*
A: Well, my job is to go to the body, basically, and not specifically to find a weapon. However, there was no weapon on him.

Q: *Did you know who Willie Dobson was?*
A: Yes.

Q: *How long have you known Willie Dobson?*
A: Five or six years.

Q: *Did you socialize with him?*
A: No.

Q: *Did you know him in a professional capacity?*
A: Yes.

Q: *Had you ever arrested him?*
A: I believe so, yes.

Q: *Based upon your personal knowledge of Willie Dobson, did you expect to find a weapon on him or near him?*
A: Yes.

Q: *Do you know Roger Ligon?*
A: No, I do not.

Q: *Did you subsequently learn of his reputation in the community?*
A: Yes, I did.

Q: *And what is that reputation?*
A: It was outstanding.

Generally, evidence of a criminal defendant's reputation cannot be introduced by the prosecution *unless* the defense raises the issue. At that point, the prosecution is allowed to show evidence of his bad character, which is usually devastating. Everything I had learned about Roger suggested that nobody would have a bad thing to say about him. More important, every cop seemed to have the highest opinion of him. Why not use the State's witnesses to lay that foundation?

Detective Corsello continued:

Q: *When you say outstanding, is that better than good?*
A: I would say yes. I would say yes.

These were the *State's* witnesses!

I called about a dozen police officers as we started our case. I called the head of the narcotics task force, who detailed how Roger was a model citizen who helped them all the time. Other police officers spoke glowingly of Roger as well. The detectives who took his confession testified as to his cooperation and kind manner. I asked all the police officers about the victim, Willie Dobson. He was not a nice guy and was categorically considered to be very dangerous. Detective Larry Eisenstein testified as to just how dangerous Willie Dobson was.

Q: *If Willie Dobson were to say to you, "You're doomed. I'm coming back with my boys . . . You're a dead man"—how would you feel?*
A: I would take him very seriously, knowing him and the people he associated with.

Q: *But how certain would you be that he would come back and shoot you?*
A: I would be very certain.

Q: *Scale of one to ten? (I took a shot here.)*
A: (pausing) Ten!

I called two psychologists up to the stand who explained PTSD. One had treated Roger from the beginning of this case. She described his behavior and her conclusion that Roger absolutely suffered from PTSD. The second one was a combat commander from Vietnam who was now a psychologist specializing in these cases, based out of Denver. He had not met Roger but was going to examine him that evening and let us know his findings the next day. The TV people made much of this, claiming it was showmanship on my part. Whatever.

The Denver psychologist came back the next day and told the jury that Roger did suffer from PTSD. I asked him questions that would generally be the last thing a defense attorney would want to hear. In almost every case, we try to convince the jury that our clients may have done this or that, but that they *never intended* to cause the death, injury, or whatever. In this case, I asked this witness why Roger had emptied his gun into Dobson. "Because he wanted to make sure he was dead!" declared the psychologist. This is what a marine does. He shoots the enemy to kill him. I was actually asking the jury to believe that my client had intended to kill the victim. If I was going to go with the PTSD defense, I felt I had to be consistent. I wanted the jury to believe that Roger had become a marine again in that parking lot, and had believed he had to destroy the enemy in order to protect himself. Marines don't shoot people to wound them; they shoot to kill. That was the way it was, and is. The jury was educated about Vietnam, PTSD, and its symptoms. But what about Roger?

I showed the prosecutor the *Death Valley* book about Roger's company and the combat they had engaged in. Was Roger's name in the book? "Well, no, not really . . . but I think it is relevant since it clearly talks about his unit." I asked the prosecutor if he had any objection to my introducing just a few pages of the book into evidence. The prosecutor had no objection. Apart from being a very nice guy (he is now a judge), he couldn't help but like Roger. To further complicate matters, his older brother and I had been friends in high school, after which his brother became a combat commander in Vietnam.

I had seriously considered calling his older brother as an expert witness relative to the horrors of Vietnam combat. How impressed would the jury have been to hear this stuff from the prosecutor's own brother! All I could think of was the scene in *Miracle on 34th Street* when the lawyer puts the prosecutor's little boy on the stand to testify that Santa Claus really does exist . . . It was one of those ideas lawyers like me get that seem brilliant—for about twenty minutes. I soon came to my senses and concluded it would be a cheap shot to shake up the prosecutor, which the jury would recognize and fault me for. It would also take the focus off the real issues of the case.

The prosecutor allowed me to put the pages of this book into evidence. Why not? The case was still a slam dunk for the State. What difference could some book make? He could afford to be generous. I asked the clerk to read the pages to the jury, who listened as carefully as any jury I had ever seen. They were transfixed. They were soon in a jungle across the world, twenty-two years ago.

The last jet screamed over by 1400—the 12.7mm delivering a parting volley—then 2nd Platoon of K/3/7 got moving again, trudging uphill. AK47s commenced firing and everyone flopped in place as the bullets chopped the high brush above them. The fire seemed to be coming from one spot straight ahead. Lieutenant Nyulassy, who could have been no less tired than his men, was up shouting encouragement and directions, and the grunts fell into a ragged line again. They fired and threw grenades, and scrambled uphill. The NVA fire stopped; they found an abandoned bunker, a couple of spider holes, and bloodstains, but no bodies.

The squads maintained their line, then bogged down in a field of shoulder-high elephant grass. Ten meters into the briar—as the grunts were shouldering through the sharp rows of blades, increasing their frustrated exhaustion, getting disorganized in the tangle—the North Vietnamese ambushed them from higher up on the ridge.

The 12.7mm and several AK47s scythed the grass. Everyone scrambled for cover. . . . the 12.7mm kept firing . . . keeping the platoon pinned.

Lance Corporal Jose Francisco Jimenez, a small, wiry fireteam leader, got up. No one had ordered him to. He simply crashed through the elephant grass, rushing uphill right into a North Vietnamese, who popped from a spider hole to shoot him. Jimenez cut him down in an instant with his M16, then was upon two more of them. He blew them away in their spider holes. He was near the 12.7mm, and he dropped on the tangled slope, yanked the pins from one, two, then a third grenade, and hurled them into the spot of brush from where the gun seemed to be firing, rushing up after the explosions, firing on the run. The 12.7mm gun was in a shallow pit on a tripod, its gunner slumped dead. Lieutenant Nyulassy was on Jimenez's heels, shouting the platoon up the fifty meters to the gun pit. Then another group of AK47s screamed from the right flank. Lance Corporal Emery fired his M60 at them as Lance Corporal Jimenez charged again. He threw frags, then ran up to pump his M16 into two North Vietnamese.

In a matter of moments, Jimenez has killed six NVA regulars and silenced the machine gun. He paused for a second near the last two victims when an AK47 suddenly cracked from the left, hitting him in the side of the head. Jimenez was killed instantly.

Under the renewed fusillade, Lieutenant Nyulassy got most of his men back behind a knoll. He tried to sort out the situation. The parched elephant grass had caught fire, probably from their tracers, and burned out of control.

2nd Platoon consolidated on the slope as two squads from 1st Platoon, under Sergeant Frank, came up. . . . Sergeant Frank led his men up through the burnt patch of elephant grass. Then the wind suddenly shifted and the blaze sprang up behind, driving them forward. They stumbled confused in the smoky tangle right into the snipers' sights: two marines were killed and one was wounded in the sudden popping. They fell back, dragging their casualties, as soon as the fire burned down. . . .

Nyulassy got in radio contact with an aerial observer in a Bronco, who fired white phosphorous rockets along the ridge. They exploded in a smokescreen of thick, white clouds, and the marines raised a cacophony of M16, M60, and M79 fire as another team rushed forward. *Jimenez's body was on fire; a grunt got close enough to grab him, but Jimenez tore loose in his hands* [emphasis added].

Six marines were dead, nine wounded . . . Lance Corporal Jose Francisco Jimenez—from Mexico City, nicknamed JoJo—was posthumously awarded the Congressional Medal of Honor.

It was time for the next witness. Who could follow that reading?

"Ronald Frank," I calmly announced. On cue, the door opened and Sergeant Frank emerged from the pages of that book and walked into the courtroom and back into the life of Roger Ligon. He was there to rescue another one of his marines. Sergeant Frank and Roger stared at each other. They had not seen each other since the day of that firefight.

I asked Sergeant Frank if he had read the book. He said he had not been aware of it until I'd shown it to him after having tracked him down. He recounted that day and the horror of losing six men while trying to recover JoJo's body.

"Why would you do that?" I asked, truly ignorant of the obvious but moving response.

"The marines don't leave their dead, sir." This was easily the most silent moment I have ever experienced in a courtroom, and probably most anywhere else.

The last question. "Who was the 'grunt' that grabbed JoJo, only to have the flesh tear loose from the bone?"

"That was Roger Ligon." The words were not spoken so much as choked from his throat. Sergeant Frank and Roger Ligon were both crying at that moment, as were several jurors . . . and the judge. No cross-examination by the prosecutor. He was moved as well, and could not bring himself to even begin to cast any shadow on this man. I believe this was a testament to his prosecutorial skills, as well as the high measure of his character.

As Frank stood up to leave the stand, I asked the judge if I could ask him a couple more questions, which I had forgotten to ask during the direct examination. (Not really, of course.)

Q: *I have one question: What do you do for a living?*
A: I'm a Sheriff's Deputy—Albany County Sheriff's Office in Laramie.

Q: *You're a Deputy Sheriff?*
A: Yes sir.

Q: *Is that a law enforcement officer?*
A: Yes sir.

Q: *Where is that?*
A: Laramie, Wyoming

Q: *How long have you done that?*
A: Going on ten years.

Q: Nothing further.

As Sergeant Frank left the stand, he went to Roger and they embraced. Neither the prosecutor nor judge interfered.

The next witness was Lieutenant Nyulassy, now a pipe fitter in New Jersey. The same scene was played out. The tears flowed again.

Lastly, Captain Robert Pendoley took the stand. He was Roger's commanding officer from day one in Vietnam. He described how

Roger was just a happy young man when he had arrived, and how the terror of these experiences seemed to change him. Pendoley was now the city planner for San Rafael, California. These three white men had come across the country, at their own expense, to tell this jury who Roger Ligon was.

I had never told Roger that I had found these men and that they would be coming to court. I wanted the jury to see his reaction and shock when it occurred. Overly dramatic? A bit contrived? I plead guilty—with an (obvious) explanation: It was tremendously effective.

My last witness was Roger Ligon. Most lawyers would successfully argue that I would be guilty of malpractice by putting my client on the stand when our defense was PTSD, a form of insanity. The more articulate, rational, or sensible he might appear to the jury, the more it would seem to defeat our defense theory. I didn't care. These people had to get to know who Roger was, and why the police, the community, and these brave veterans had all lined up to help him.

Roger had joined the marines in 1968 because he liked the uniform. He really didn't know much about Vietnam, or that he might be sent there. He was a bit overweight and failed the harsh basic training regimen at Parris Island the first time, so he did it again. He passed, and soon found himself in Southeast Asia. When he came home, people made fun of him for being a sucker and serving his country. Although he had once been so proud of his uniform, he stopped wearing it because of the cruel treatment he received from some insensitive morons with whom he worked. He married and raised two very lovely children. He also helped put his nieces and nephews through school. He then described the effects of PTSD and how he could not walk into the woods without smelling blood. He needed the alcohol to sleep. He just wasn't the same.

He told us of that day in August of 1989 when Willie Dobson said he was coming back "with his boys" to kill Roger, and that he was "a dead man." Roger had believed him. He became a marine again and did what he had to do. The jury had learned from those combat chronologies that the North Vietnamese "boys" would come into their camps with unexploded ammunition for which they would be paid a bounty. Often, however, they would be there as a ruse, and would explode a grenade, killing or wounding the unsuspecting marines. Would the jury appreciate the connection? Roger deeply regretted what he had done. He said he prayed for forgiveness every day. The prosecutor did his best to hammer Roger into admitting that he knew exactly what he was doing every moment. Roger always gave the same (and unrehearsed) answer. "I dunno . . . my head was empty."

The State called a psychiatrist to try and blow away our insanity defense. It backfired. On cross-examination, the shrink told the jury that although Roger wasn't insane, he was a very good man who had been threatened by a very bad man. This was a tragedy, he said, "and why I told the prosecutor to make a plea bargain or something so nothing bad would happen to Roger."

The jury deliberated for three days. The foreperson finally announced their verdict of not guilty, with tears running down her cheeks. (Her husband was a Vietnam veteran.)

Connecticut, like most states, allows people to be found not guilty by reason of insanity, or "mental disease or defect." What most people do not understand is that such a finding is generally *not* a win. The person acquitted is not freed. They are immediately committed to a mental health facility where they stay until doctors find that they are no longer a threat to themselves or the community. In Connecticut, the average amount of time such an acquitted homicide defendant spends in this type of facility is about twenty-nine years. Had Roger pled guilty to manslaughter, or even murder, he would probably have been facing no more than twenty-five years.

Roger spent exactly forty-five days in the mental health facility. The folks in charge could not see any reason to keep him there, and they had the courage to say so. I was there with his family when he walked out. Second to the birth of my children, I cannot remember a more rewarding moment in my life. About a week after his release, he dropped by my office. He wanted to give me something. There was never any money in this case other than what his boss and the vets put together, which was used up pretty quickly, paying the experts. But this was never about money. Roger gave me his Purple Heart from Vietnam. Like O. Henry's "The Gift of the Magi," it was his treasure, and he wanted me to have it.

The prosecutor in the case, Bruce Hudock, is now one of the best judges in our state. He presides with the same common sense, compassion, and kindness that was so apparent in the Ligon trial.

Roger Ligon, who had never been in trouble in his life before that day, remains a model citizen. I see him all the time. If there is a benefit for an injured police officer, Roger Ligon is there. He truly is a citizen of the world. Recently, he was a guest at my wedding, and I continued to win on this case when his daughter asked me to be godfather to her newborn son, Treyvon Jones. It doesn't get any better than that. The message of the Ligon case is important. When we read about some crime in the paper or see it in the "crawl" on CNN, we do not know the whole story. Everyone *looks* guilty! It is just the nature of the media coverage. Willie Dow, a terrific lawyer in Connecticut, said it best at a lecture he and I gave about the inherent bias in the media coverage of alleged crimes: "When is the last time you looked at the newspaper and said, 'Wow—this guy must be innocent!' "

The Ligon case seemed undefendable to most people, including me. More cynically, I had prejudged Roger Ligon as being someone who didn't deserve a good defense. How jaded and burned out could I have been to be so ready to write someone off because of my take on the crappy headline and the biased story in the news? I learned that we defense lawyers don't have all the answers, nor are we always the best judges of human conduct. We have to take several steps back from our cases and our clients at times. We are often better off being a *mensch* than a super lawyer.

{Chapter 12}

You're On
Unless the Pope Dies:
TV Lawyering

In Woody Allen's film *Deconstructing Harry*, his character is in an elevator descending to the various depths, or floors, of hell. The doors open and we hear, "Level 27—serial killers and lawyers who appear on TV!"

Who are these people? Where did we come from, and what makes us experts on whatever happened that afternoon in Yakima? Clearly, the blame rests with Steve Brill, who invented Court TV and invited us to be his free talent to comment on the trials that he began televising in July of 1990. We sat in his studio for four hours at a clip, pontificating on the trials of William Kennedy Smith, Betty Broderick, the Menendez brothers, and then the Holy Grail, the Trial of O.J. Simpson. Other networks and shows soon hit the airwaves, and before long, it became virtually impossible to avoid the banter of angry ex-prosecutors and feisty defense lawyers, no matter how fast you were with a clicker. During the O.J. Simpson case, more people than were willing to admit it made sure they were home by 9:00 p.m. EST to watch Geraldo and his panel on CNBC's *Rivera Live*.

The producers and bookers for these shows reached out to the Court TV stable at first, and then began filling their own Rolodexes, and later on, BlackBerries, with the lawyers who were involved in these big cases. They found lawyers who had written books, were famous for something or other, or who just looked really good on TV.

I am often asked by lawyers how they can get on TV. In fact, I have actually given speeches on this topic. I explain that the producers/bookers will call them if they are an expert on some issue that might be hot by reason of a big case currently in the news. They can also get on TV if they are involved in some big case. The only other way they are going to get that call is if somebody like me feeds their name to the bookers. This always brings a smile to the group—they're as good as seated in the limo to CNN! Within days they will be staring at Larry King's suspenders, leaning over that table, chatting like old fraternity brothers.

I explain to them that after my little speech, several of them will ask for my card, e-mail address, or whatever, so they can send me their clippings, briefs, headshots, and résumés for me to pass on to the networks. I tell them that when they do, I will be very affable, encouraging them to send me all that crap. But I also tell them that I am lying! Why do I want to share this deal with them? Who needs the competition of other lawyers! I am going to throw their stuff in the garbage. So, in other words, don't bother. Without exception, every time I have given this incredibly candid speech, including the shabby warning, several people *still* eagerly come up to me and send me their stuff. Such is the allure of television.

At least for the entertainment value, let me run through the process.

You got the call! Somehow your name came up on their contact file or Rolodex, and there is a producer/booker on the phone about to ask you some questions. A booker is a young person whose job it is to find a warm body to be in their studio at 4:15 P.M. to talk to whomever about some case or legal issue. A producer is basically the same person with a slightly bigger cubbyhole in the studio's newsroom or basement. I'm pretty sure their jobs are the same, except the producers get to holler at the bookers.

First, understand that Jennifer (they are generally named Jennifer) is probably not as old as most of the shoes in your closet. Thus, your erudite references to Watergate or the Scopes Monkey Trial will not play that well. Your energy level must immediately knock her over! (This is not hard to learn. Just tune in to the Game Show Network on cable TV and watch any of the contestants on *The Dating Game* from the '70s.) Their next priority will be whether or not you have any expertise or experience in the case or issue that is the subject of the segment. This is the easiest part. For example, a typical question is: "Have you ever represented any lesbian shepherds for counterfeiting?"

"I have three cases like that coming up for trial, and two on appeal!"

That's right—you exaggerate a bit! This is cable television, not a federal grand jury. In the four minutes you will be on, you can wing it! Now comes the tricky part. They will want to know "where you stand on this issue," whatever issue that might be. If you are a prosecutor, or "former prosecutor," it will be assumed that you want every law enforced to the ultimate degree, and that anyone who has been arrested is a scumbag who is certainly guilty. We defense people have a bit more latitude. One reason for this is that 99 percent of us are all "former prosecutors" as well.

So here's the deal: You have to figure out what they need for this show. They generally want to see us bicker and fight, within the bounds of dignity, unless some really great backbiting occurs, which might rival a pre-fight interview with two professional wrestlers. Before Jennifer asks you where you weigh in on this case, you immediately interrupt her by innocently asking, "So who else is on this show?" When she tells you that she has booked the ranting, perpetually angry ex-prosecutor who feels that all counterfeiters should be castrated, you then know she needs someone to unconditionally defend whomever. You immediately spring into a short speech on how lesbian shepherds have been the most maligned minority on the face of the planet. In fact, you were the keynote speaker at their last convention! (Okay—that might be a little much, but you get the picture.) Jennifer is elated.

The last question is the most important: Can you be in New York City or in front of a camera at some local studio at 7:00 P.M. tonight?

Panic time. Your daughter's class play, wife's birthday dinner, or your preparation for tomorrow's colonoscopy all pose a serious conflict. But this is television. Live television! They will surely understand.

You are "booked." Another Jennifer will be calling you soon for the "pre-interview." But then again, are you "soft-booked" or "hard-booked"? They won't tell you. *Soft-booked* means they love you and you are definitely on the show—unless another Jennifer comes up with somebody better. *Hard-booked* means they are probably not going to call anyone else, and you will be on television unless something else happens, as discussed below. They will send a limo for you, and you will be on at 7:12 P.M. that night. You immediately call all of your friends and relatives. VCRs are programmed and everyone will TiVo you.

In the green room at the studio you are treated to some donuts that were very fresh during the network's early morning show. They pat you down with makeup and then spray your hair with Elmer's glue so there are no fly-aways. For some reason, the hair people at these networks must lose their jobs and become forever blacklisted if any strand of your hair is sticking up while you are on the show. To make sure that doesn't happen, they plaster your hair down flat like Rudolph Valentino.

You sit in the green room watching the TV monitor. Other guests for other shows come in to wait for their segments. You soon find yourself chatting with Dr. Ruth, Henry Kissinger, a shark attack victim, and a lady who owns an Oreo cookie with the image of the Virgin Mary on it. A sound guy comes in and gropes you all over as he sticks a plastic thing in your ear and tapes a wire to your jacket, connected to a speaker. You are minutes away from following in the footsteps of Edward R. Murrow. You are wondering if those morons who crapped on you in high school will be watching!

Then disaster strikes. You sit there in disbelief as the station switches to breaking news in some small town in South Carolina. There is an Amber Alert for a young girl who has apparently been abducted by her father, who looks like Billy Ray Cyrus. The local police chief is about to hold a news conference. Your big break is about to be eclipsed and preempted by this chief's long-awaited moment in the sun. The chief drones on, thanking all of his deputies and answering the probing questions of the national media folks (who seem to get to these places faster than Superman when a story breaks). Moments later, the girl is found safe. Her dad got pissed off at her mother and kidnapped her for the afternoon to take her to Denny's. The crisis is over and the satellite trucks are back on the road. But sadly for you, your moment has come . . . and gone.

Jennifer's coworker, Jason, comes out to tell you that they have to cancel your segment, but "they will call you again real soon." The sound guy is yanking the thing out of your ear. The wires are being ripped from your chest. You frantically clutch that donut! Then you start thinking about all your family and friends who are even now watching Chief Brady as he explains how brilliant his deputies are. What will they think? You have plenty of time to mull this over during the very long ride home in the limo.

Recently, I sat on the set of a cable news studio with three other lawyers, ready to discuss something fairly significant, like whether or not the current attorney general should be fired. We all had our clippings from *The New York Times* together with other research we had done ourselves, or were given by Jennifer's coworker, Jason, who is chained to a computer somewhere downstairs in the bowels of the studio. Our segment was going to be pretty lengthy—a half hour. That is an eternity in the world of TV lawyers.

And then Champ got stuck in the mud. I am totally serious. Some big stupid horse in Mississippi fell into some big mud hole and we went "live" to Mississippi, where this horse was moving around in this big hole while a dozen people with ropes and machines tried to figure out how to get him out. My colleagues and I sat there like schmucks for the entire thirty minutes, all decked out in our makeup, hair glued down, watching the horse on the monitor and listening to some veterinarian that Jennifer got on the phone telling us what to expect and such. What was incredible to me was that the anchor, Martha MacCallum at Fox News, had a million truly relevant questions to ask the vet and the folks who were trying to get the horse out of the mud. I mean, how do you come up with more than, "So, what are they gonna do?" in this situation. Martha carried the entire half hour expertly, without missing a beat. We got bumped by Champ!

Knowing the unpredictability of these TV bookings, I often try and get a feel from Jennifer if they are really going to air the segment, or if they are just teeing me up in case they lose the satellite feed from Encino where a guy in a tank top in a stolen SUV has led the police on a 68-mile wild car chase. I once got the best message from the network after I'd called them, trying to learn if they really were going to use me that night. "Hi, Mickey—this is Jennifer. You're on unless the pope dies!"

• • •

As I mentioned earlier, walking into a cable news station green room can be a very interesting experience. I once found myself in the green room at Fox News, battling a group of seven fortyish people for the Krispy Kreme donuts. I always try and figure out who the people are, or what their hook is that's getting them airtime on TV. This crew was a mystery to me. They weren't political people. A few of them had accents. They had a couple of handlers with them who seemed like publicists. As they walked onto the set, I asked a producer. Turns out they were the cast from the original *Willy Wonka & the Chocolate Factory* movie; they were on tour promoting the twenty-fifth anniversary of the film, which was being rereleased as a director's cut. Seeing them was much better than exchanging pleasantries with the Speaker of the House or any one of those sixty-seven annoying blonde "Republican strategists."

Waiting in the green room can be a bit boring. Combine that fact with my ADD and there can be trouble. I was in some green room waiting to go on to talk about the Natalee Holloway case wherein that poor girl from Alabama disappeared in Aruba. There was a tall, nice-looking man sitting by himself reading the newspaper. I introduced myself and asked him what story he was there for. With a distinct Dutch accent he told me he was a homicide detective from Amsterdam. "Can I ask you a question?"

'Sure. . . . Vhata would you like to know?" he answered in a very dignified Dutch accent.

My book was way upside down at this point. "When you are following a suspect, don't they hear those wooden shoes behind them?"

Thankfully, the local Jennifer grabbed him right then to bring him onto the set.

The measure of a good booker at these networks is determined by whom they can get. The first choice is always somebody connected to the case that is the subject of the segment. Starting with the accused or the victim, there is an exponential search for lesser involved people like witnesses, neighbors, friends, not-so-good friends, and so forth and so on. You must appreciate that someone's ability to speak on camera in any cogent manner is *not* one of the search criteria. This can often make for some very painful interviews of people who are classic "deer caught in the headlights." They cannot seem to remember their own names before they become tongue-tied when asked what kind of neighbor Jimmy James Johnson was before he was arrested for God knows what.

Occasionally there are genius bookings. My favorite one concerned the recent plight of actor/director Mel Gibson. We all felt his pain, but somehow couldn't watch enough of his misery, which ruled the airwaves for a couple of weeks after he made some anti-Semitic comments during a DWI arrest in California. The bookers gave us the usual suspects. The cable news (and network news) bookers gave us anti-defamation people and various rabbis to tell us whether the Jewish people could ever forgive Mel. Hollywood publicists and spin experts told us how many times Mel should apologize and to whom. Some cops came on to tell us how wacky people can get when they get pulled over for DWI. Lawyers like me opined about whether the cops were unfair to him, and what would happen to him in the courthouse. I did manage to get in some of my own clients' DWI experiences. (One of my clients took the breath test and was three times the limit. The officer told him that he was under arrest because he was legally drunk. "Wait," he said. "If I'm *legally* drunk, where's the problem, Officer?") Even Al Sharpton got some serious airtime.

By the second week of this drama, the bookers were running low on "Mel's a schmuck" talent. I was in the green room at Fox News, but I wasn't there for that story. I have totally forgotten what I was there to talk about. There was a nice-looking, very athletic guy sitting there with an attractive woman. He didn't look like a terrorism expert or some politico. I asked him what segment he was there to talk about. "Mel Gibson," he calmly replied, and then turned his attention back to the lady. I was clearly annoying him. A producer came in to bring him out to the set. I watched with great interest, since I pride myself on guessing what people are there to talk about. I had no clue what his hook was in this story.

When he was introduced, I clapped loudly in appreciation of this booking, again annoying everyone in the green room. (Annoying people in the green room is obviously my "signature move.") Who was this guy? Well, apparently he was Atlanta Braves superstar John Rocker, who had made big-time news in New York and pretty much everywhere in January of 2000, when, in an interview with *Sports Illustrated*, he was quoted as saying:

[New York City is] the most hectic, nerve-wracking city. Imagine having to take the 7 train to the ballpark, looking like you're riding through Beirut next to some kid with purple hair, next to some queer with AIDS, right next to some dude who just got out of jail for the fourth time, right next to some 20-year-old mom with four kids. It's depressing.

Supposedly, Rocker had some history of being less than kind when referring to some minorities, but essentially giving the finger to the New York City baseball fans brought him an avalanche of bad press and ill feeling. On *The Tonight Show*, Jay Leno had guests hit a John Rocker dummy with baseball bats. *Saturday Night Live* did a great skit on him. He eventually apologized and served his penance by meeting with legendary Hank Aaron and former Atlanta mayor and civil rights pioneer Andrew Young. So why was he on TV talking about Mel Gibson? In an absolutely brilliant move, somebody at Fox had obviously said to themselves, "Let's see . . . Who can we get who has made incredibly moronic statements in the past . . . ?" I would love to have heard the call they made.

Borrowing the comedy stylings of comedian Bob Newhart, per his shtick on *The Ed Sullivan Show*, I have to believe the phone call went something like this:

(Newhart would only do one side of the conversation.)

Hello, Mr. Rocker; this is Jason from Fox News, and we are doing a show about Mel Gibson. We'd love to have you on.

Yes, I understand you don't know Mr. Gibson.

Yes, I know you're not Jewish.

Yes, I understand that you don't know much about what happened.

Well, we believe you could really add a lot to the program.

Well, yes, that's right . . . We believe that since you kind of went through this same kind of experience when you said those things about New York City, which you clearly did not mean . . .

What amazed me is that Rocker agreed to come on the show to talk about what it is like to say really stupid stuff that offends a lot of people. How stupid could this guy be? I could not have been more wrong. He was one of the best guests I have ever seen. On camera, he readily agreed that, like Gibson, he had run off at the mouth and made statements that were offensive to a great many people. He totally conceded that he was wrong to have done it, and that he regretted it. More important, he then very logically asked why everyone places so much importance on the comments of actors or sports stars. "We are basically circus performers; why would anyone be so concerned about our opinions or comments?" I'm probably not doing justice to his interview. He was extremely articulate and made total sense about the way we tend to overvalue the ramblings of celebrities. That was a genius booking. Great job, Jennifer or Jason!

• • •

Now, while I have made TV bookings sound fascinating and glamorous thus far, there is a dark and dangerous truth to them as well: Sometimes you *are* on television even when you're *not* on television. This may sound silly, but here's the deal: When you are in a TV studio and you have a microphone on your clothes, people are often both watching and listening to you! I am talking about when you are sitting there on the set during commercials, in the green room before the show, or when you are in some tiny "headshot" studio in Yakima or Baltimore, doing a "remote" interview.

At the beginning of the O.J. trial coverage, I was sitting with Geraldo Rivera on the set of CNBC's *Rivera Live*. One of the great secrets of cable television is how decent a guy Geraldo Rivera really is. He often gets a bad rap for absurd reasons. As with any TV personality, if you want to know whether they are a good guy or an asshole, ask the sound person or the hair and makeup people, or other members of the crew. That is the true litmus test for any TV personality, and Geraldo passes with flying colors.

As the O.J. show got under way, one of the guests made a statement that I thought was really stupid. He was sitting in a studio in L.A., and I could see him clearly on one of the monitors in our studio in Fort Lee, New Jersey. He was a well-known journalist, so I wasn't about to call him a schmuck on TV—I just politely disagreed. After we broke for the commercial, I turned to Geraldo and calmly said, "Is this guy a fuckin' asshole or what!" From the monitor, the journalist said, "You know—I don't appreciate that comment, Mr. Sherman!" Who knew he could hear me?

When Martha Stewart was about to surrender herself at Danbury Prison, I was waiting to talk about it in the green room at Fox News. I was appearing on *The Big Story with Rita Cosby*, and I had neglected to ask who else would be appearing on the show. I started channel surfing on the TV in the green room, where I knew I would eventually find someone sitting in front of a camera, staring into TV nothingness, waiting for his or her moment in the sun. Those of us who have been doing this a while know that there are people watching to see if we will pick our noses or spit on our hands to fix our hair, like a famous politician did last year. Sometimes there will be a guest who is an absolute pain in the ass to the crew, and you can watch them endlessly complaining about the sound and the lighting, the lack of fresh coffee, or whatever. Green-room channel surfing for these unsuspecting folks certainly qualifies as some form of voyeurism, but I recommend it to anyone who wants to be entertained before finding out if they have been bumped by a slow-speed car chase in Encino.

I found the other Martha Stewart "expert" sitting alone in a studio somewhere. He was staring into the camera silently. All of a sudden, his face became animated and he almost shouted, "Hello, Rita!" I looked at the monitor that showed current programming, and Rita's show wasn't on yet. I flipped back to this guy. "Hi, Rita . . . *Hey*, Rita . . . Good *evening*, Rita . . . *Hello* there, Rita!" (with a Stone Phillips–ish head tilt). He was practicing his salutation. Then he began rehearsing his responses to whatever questions he thought

Rita would be asking him. "Well, Danbury Prison is going to get their most famous prisoner in years tomorrow afternoon!" He practiced that one about eight times.

Who was this guy? Obviously he had never been on TV before and was trying to rehearse his lines. It appeared I was going to be on the same segment. My plan was to try and get the first comment out; I planned to say, "Well, Danbury Prison is going to get their most famous prisoner in years tomorrow afternoon!" I was going to steal his line! What would he do? This was going to be great! I was brought out onto the set, microphone stuck on my lapel. Rita kisses me hello, and we're on. They introduce me, and then this other guy, from his remote location. As I take a deep breath to get ready to screw up his line, I glance at the guy's title on the screen.

FRANK BROWN

MEDIA EXPERT AND CONSULTANT

I was laughing so hard, I blew my chance of screwing up his opening line.

There is one valuable lesson to be learned from Mr. Brown: Always be prepared to give a great answer to a certain specific question. What if they don't ask you that question? No problem—just ask it yourself. I have done this many, many times. It always works.

Q: *Mr. Sherman, how can you justify allowing teenage drunk drivers to go free after they kill and maim people on the road?*

A: This is a difficult issue, Rita (Dan, Geraldo, Katie), but isn't the better question, "What can we do to make sure bars and liquor stores don't give our kids alcohol, which puts us *all* in harm's way?"

Okay, it *is* a bit sleazy, but it still makes good TV, and that's what really counts. This sidestepping or question substitution is best demonstrated in the movie *Animal House*, where the Delta Tau Delta fraternity is on trial for various misdeeds, including having a toga party. After the long list of infractions is rattled off, Otter stands up and declares that any criticism of his fraternity is the same as blaming the fraternity system as a whole, and faulting the entire fraternity system is the same as indicting the entire American education system, and "say what you will about the Delta house, but we won't stand for anyone trying to put down THE UNITED STATES OF AMERICA!" The Delta house members walk out of the room with great pride. (I guess it speaks volumes about my oratory skills, or lack thereof, that I rely on the movie *Animal House* to advocate for my causes on television.)

We can't all be Alan Dershowitz; I know I'm not. That is why I tend to take this whole TV lawyer thing a lot less seriously than perhaps I should. In fact, it is fairly certain that I will not be tapped to anchor the ABC nightly news, or any other news show, for that matter. And I really don't make my living doing these shows. The donuts and limo rides really can't pay the mortgage. So, why not have as much fun as possible without insulting the viewers or pissing off the networks . . . too much.

Years ago I was on some show discussing a big case involving a constitutional issue, which was light years over my head and even further from my interest. To my dismay, instead of having one of the screaming blonde ex-prosecutors to spar with, professor Alan Dershowitz was in the big box on the upper right of the screen, explaining the case and finishing with an erudite quote from "Justice Jackson." The anchor then looked to me for my response.

I went for it. "What you talkin' 'bout, Willis?"

The camera and sound crew laughed very loudly. I was encouraged.

"I guess the difference between myself and Professor Dershowitz is that while he cites Justice Jackson of the Supreme Court, I rely on *Arnold* Jackson of *Diff'rent Strokes*." I think that is the last time I was on TV with Alan Dershowitz.

Very recently, the reigning Miss America, together with John Walsh, who created the incredibly effective program *America's Most Wanted*, assisted the police department in trapping some online child sex predators. The twenty-year-old beauty queen from Oklahoma worked with the police department in Suffolk County, New York, to target internet sexual predators while taping an episode of *America's Most Wanted*. Miss America posed as a teenager, lured some men into chatting online with her, and convinced them to meet her at a house where both the police and TV crew were waiting for the suckers. Eleven men were arrested in this sting operation. These kinds of charges are extraordinarily serious and it is rare that the offenders do *not* go to prison.

Sounds like a win-win. But somehow, Miss America made it known to somebody, who told the whole world (or at least the cable news networks, which is the same thing) that she may not really want to testify in court. Soon Suffolk County District Attorney Thomas Spota released the following statement to *Newsday*: "Her agents have told us that she's not coming back to testify." Her agents! How pissed off was the district attorney's office?! The shit hit the fan. The Jennifers rounded up all the TV lawyers to weigh in on this vitally important legal issue: Should Miss America be forced to testify?

I was on a Fox News panel with the usual suspects: political guy, victims' rights zealot, and a former federal prosecutor who also happens to be my wife, Lis Wiehl. Wendy, the victims' rights advocate, screamed at me as usual, blaming the slimy defense lawyers for everything, including Hurricane Katrina. The political guy kind of just sold his latest book about God knows what. (He had obviously read my lecture above, about ignoring the question and putting out only the information he wanted to!) Lis gave her typical calm, reasoned, Barnard/Harvard, totally correct answer. "Of course Miss America will testify . . ." I agreed with Lis, but added that I also believed she "would testify in a swimsuit, playing 'Lady of Spain' on the accordion while outlining how she would achieve world peace." Lis moved her chair a bit further away from me.

"But what if she does *not* testify?" asked the Fox News anchor, trying to maintain some measure of legitimacy and relevance to this hot topic. I jumped in. I didn't go to Columbia or Harvard, but I *knew* the answer to this one and couldn't wait to share my genius with the viewing public. "If she doesn't testify, or cannot testify"—pausing to make sure the camera was squarely on me—"then the first runner-up would testify in her place. Am I the only one who knows the rules around here?"

• • •

Nancy Grace was a very aggressive prosecutor in Georgia when she was hired away by Court TV years ago. She is notoriously pro-prosecution, and many defense lawyers bad-mouth her for her views and her frequent castigation of people like me, who appear on her CNN show very frequently. I disagree with my defense comrades. I like Nancy. I appreciate the way in which she has so totally (and apparently, very sincerely) invented herself, and will not be dissuaded from her victim-oriented mission. She got a real bad rap recently when she laid into twenty-one-year-old Melinda Duckett, whose two-year-old son went missing. Nancy cross-examined her live on the air and, in my opinion, was totally within her rights to ask the tough questions of a woman whose responses would have convinced anyone that she was the killer. Shortly after the interview, Melinda Duckett took her own life. The media tried to make Nancy the bad guy, and it wasn't fair. I rarely agree with her about cases, but, as the credo goes, I defend her right to say whatever she wants to. This doesn't mean I can't have fun with her. She is also a good friend and appreciates and tolerates my humor.

I sat in the little CNN studio doing her show recently. There was a gaggle of other "experts" dealing with various aspects of this terrible case we were discussing. Apparently the authorities had dug up sixteen bodies in some guy's front yard in the South (or the Midwest—I can't recall). Naturally, he wore a tank top. Anyone who has watched more than one episode of *Cops* or any of those "America's Most Insane, Scary, Moronic High-Speed Car Chases" that run continuously on TV, knows that if tank tops were outlawed, the national crime rate would plummet.

Back to the CNN studio, where Nancy Grace is showing video of this guy's front lawn with all the dug-up graves. He was being charged with multiple counts of murder, rape, sodomy, and kidnapping. At some point I knew the little red light was going to come on atop the camera pointed at me, and I was going to have to come out with some classic but hackneyed TV lawyer line, like, "Well, Nancy, they still have to connect the dots . . . ." (The FCC has ruled that any TV lawyer who does *not* use the "connect the dots" line at least once a month may not appear on TV again for a year.)

"Defahnse lahhwyer Mickey Sherman, how would you defend this guy?" Nancy asked.

I went with the next-best cliché. "You know, Nancy, we see this all the time. The police come by and dig up fifteen, sixteen bodies in my client's front yard, and all of the sudden . . . there is this"—making the air-quotes gesture—"rush to judgment that my client is guilty of something. Nancy, these cops are out of control!"

We went directly to commercial.

The "rush to judgment" thing has been around for a long time, but most of us credit the O.J. trial for making it a brand name that we all feel compelled to use every ten minutes, in court and in studios. The third obligatory TV lawyer cliché is: "Well, they can't put the ketchup back in the bottle." I have always wondered about that one. Someone put the ketchup in the bottle in the first place, so . . . .

Not too long ago, Duane "Dog" Chapman, the very famous bounty hunter from Hawaii, was arrested in Mexico. He went there and kidnapped escaped serial rapist Andrew Luster, whom the FBI and state authorities could not seem to find. Dog found him in Mexico, sent him back to the USA, and then got jailed by the Mexican authorities for breaking their laws by kidnapping somebody. Something just didn't compute here. He certainly did a good deed, yet was still held in a really crappy Mexican jail for a while. The day he got out, I saw him on some newscast. He was wearing wraparound sunglasses, apparently because he was: a) given a black eye by some thug in jail; b) just very cool; or c) both of the above.

That evening I was scheduled to appear on Fox News's *Big Story*, where we would be talking about Dog and his plight. He popped up on the monitor from Texas or someplace, wearing the glasses. The question to me was whether or not he should return to Mexico to face the charges. Invoking my "I ain't no Dershowitz" credo, I opined that he shouldn't even go out for Mexican food, much less go back to Mexico. More important, I wore wraparound sunglasses to show my support for the Dog.

Attention Deficit Disorder, an inappropriate sense of humor, and a good working knowledge of what pisses off viewers can sometimes make for some entertaining television. Using these great resources I once spent a couple of hours on Court TV with anchor and close friend Rikki Klieman. The trial we were commenting on was about some cop who shot his neighbor's dog for some stupid reason. I rarely prepare any comments before such a show since:

A. It is generally a "live" show.

B. I rarely prepare for anything.

This time, however, I knew exactly what I was going to say. I just needed the opening and Rikki served it up.

"So, will this defendant be able to get a fair trial?" Rikki asked.

"The problem is, Rikki, that everyone loves dogs. . . that's why I was so surprised when you told me during the commercial that you hate dogs. . . ."

"THAT'S A LIE!" she declared. Staring at the camera, in absolute shock and terror, Rikki then launched into a five minute sob story about the two beagles she raised a hundred years ago. As I just sat there and giggled, she pleaded with the Court TV viewers to believe her and not send her the obligatory hate e-mails that would come after such a revelation. Most lawyers take great pride in winning some technical appeal or argument before a high court. Not me. This was one of my finer moments.

A few years ago, I was invited to appear on Catherine Crier's show on Court TV. It was Halloween night, and she was hosting the show from the Scott Peterson trial. I would be in the New York studio with another guest. The show opened and she introduced her guests. I did the normal half-nod to the camera as she introduced me. You really don't have time to say hello, but you have to move some part of your body to show the producers and the viewers that you are not in a coma. But then again, it was Halloween. That is why I quickly donned the "scream" mask when I saw the camera was going to come to me.

Catherine was not looking at her TV monitor as I politely nodded hello, and only saw it as she was introducing the next guest, during which she almost lost it. Being the pro that she is, however, she came right back with, "Mickey . . . you're scary without a mask on."

I took the mask off and we talked about the murder of Laci Peterson. Cheap sight gags always make for better television journalism. Edward R. Murrow must be spinning in his grave.

How Can I
Continue to Defend
Those People?

I MENTIONED EARLIER that people like me, criminal defense attorneys, make the worst judges because we have heard just about all the bullshit stories imaginable from our clients. So why do we keep going back for more with that KICK ME sign on our butts? We often feel burned out and very much like the mythical king Sisyphus, the Greek schnook who was condemned to ceaselessly roll a big rock to the tip of a mountain where it would fall back over on him just as he thought he got it to the top. The practice of criminal defense is not unlike that scene. We battle for our clients, an ordeal that is so often a hopeless, uphill battle. Even though we know that rock is going to fall back on us, we still pull out all stops as to prevent it from happening. We rarely get paid a lot of money to go through this process. We do it because we have been conditioned to stand between our client and whatever misery may await them if their lawyer screws up. Most of us are like idiot savants—this is all we know how to do, and this is all we want to do. Why? Just remember the words of the busboy at the pizza restaurant the night I won an acquittal for a math teacher charged with sexual assault: "You're Sherman! You saved a man's life today!"

End of discussion.

{Index}

{About the Author}

MICKEY SHERMAN is a criminal defense attorney who is also the legal analyst for CBS-TV and a frequent media commentator on legal issues for all the major networks. He has appeared on *The Today Show*, *20/20*, *Larry King Live*, and scores of other national programs. He has written extensively for legal publications and has lectured around the country on criminal law issues as well as the media coverage of them. This is his first book.